Indians, Alcohol, and the Roads to Taos and Santa Fe

Indians, Alcohol, and the Roads to Taos and Santa Fe

William E. Unrau

University Press of Kansas

Published by the University Press of Kansas (Lawrence, Kansas 66045), which was organized by the Kansas Board of Regents and is operated and funded by Emporia State University, Fort Hays State University, Kansas State University, Pittsburg State University, the University of Kansas, and Wichita State University

Library of Congress Cataloging-in-Publication Data

Unrau, William E., 1929–
Indians, alcohol, and the roads to Taos and Santa Fe / William E. Unrau.
p. cm.
Includes bibliographical references and index.
ISBN 978-0-7006-1914-6 (cloth : alk. paper)
1. Indians of North America—Alcohol use—West (U.S.) 2. Indians of North America—West (U.S.)—History—19th century. 3. Indians of North America—West (U.S.)—Social conditions. 4. Liquor industry—West (U.S.)—History—19th century. 5. Prohibition—West (U.S.)—History—19th century. 6. Indian roads—West (U.S.)—History—19th century. 7. West (U.S.)—History—19th century. I. Title.
E78.W5U565 2013
978.004'97--dc23
2012044373

British Library Cataloguing-in-Publication Data is available.

Printed in the United States of America

10 9 8 7 6 5 4 3 2 1

The paper used in this publication is recycled and contains 30 percent postconsumer waste. It is acid free and meets the minimum requirements of the American National Standard for Permanence of Paper for Printed Library Materials Z39.48-1992.

In memory of Sue

Contents

Illustrations

Maps

Photographs and Drawings

Acknowledgments

Several persons provided assistance in the identification and/or procurement of certain sources used in this study: David Halaas, Douglas Comer, David Dary, David Hayes, Coi Drummond-Gehrig, Harlan Unrau, John Carson, Seth Sumsan, Alexa Robets, and Linda Revello. Their help is very much appreciated. Special thanks go to Dennis Wheaton for his cartography and to Ranjit Arab and Larisa Martin for their assistance and guidance during the final stages of the publication process.

Indians, Alcohol, and the Roads to Taos and Santa Fe

Introduction

By 1821, the year Missouri was admitted to the Union as the twenty-fourth state, overland roads had already been established from Missouri across Mexico-claimed territory to Taos and Santa Fe. Along these routes during the next quarter century an alcohol trade thrived among Indians and whites despite federal prohibitions. This book recounts how and to what effect the alcohol trade was plied in this distant and remote region during an important period of westward U.S. expansion.

European efforts at colonization of the Western Hemisphere beginning at the end of the fifteen century led to dispossession, sickness, and premature death for Indians in North, Central, and South America. Some affected "natives" (so called by many past and contemporary historians and anthropologists) were befriended by the invaders at the outset. Some were vaccinated for smallpox, others were provided material assistance against starvation, and many were even assimilated into the mainstream of American culture. On balance, however, most American Indians were impacted in the worst way as a result of encounters with Euro-American colonizers (or, some will say, invaders) and, after more than four centuries, have continued to suffer debilitation and population decline. Historians of the subject document many shameful events, leading to a consensus that the European invasion precipitated a genuine tragedy in the Western Hemisphere. This book offers details within a specific context—alcohol and its impact on Indians along the frontier trails threading through the so-called Indian Country between Missouri and Mexico—as well as new insights into how and why things went so dreadfully wrong.

There is no lack of studies on this topic. According to a U.S. National Park Service report from 1990, more than 800 books and articles had already been published on the subject of the Santa Fe Trail, a number that has increased markedly since. Having written two books on Indian exploitation and decline in the trans-Missouri West, I decided to broaden my understanding of the opening of U.S. commerce to New Mexico in 1821 and thereafter. Specifically, I began studying how it came to pass that distilled alcohol—designated illegal under penalty of federal fines and imprisonment as a trade item for Indian peoples where the Taos and Santa Fe roads threaded westward—was in fact easily obtainable by so many resident and transient Indians.

In my first book on this topic, *White Man's Wicked Water: The Alcohol Trade and Prohibition in Indian Country, 1802–1892* (1996), I focused on the duplicity and negative aspects of a hard-drinking white culture that passed legislation prohibiting Indians from procuring alcohol in any form while ignoring similar standards for itself. In my second book dealing with the topic, *The Rise and Fall of Indian Country, 1825–1855* (2007), I looked in depth at the actual *place* where the new a standards were to be applied, as well as the legal and economic problems resulting from the government's failure to enforce the Indian Trade and Intercourse statutes passed by the U.S. Congress in 1790, 1793, 1796, 1799, 1802, and 1834 regulating commerce between Native Americans and non-Indians.

This book journeys farther by examining the alcohol trade in Indian Country after 1834, when commercial relations between the United States and Mexico were expanding after being inaugurated by William Becknell of central Missouri in 1821. Becknell and his supporters conveyed goods across an immense landscape inhabited by thousands of equestrian hunters who, in response to an increasing demand for processed bison robes and related products (which they harvested for their own needs or for bartering with other Indians at regional fairs), were induced by non-Indian traders to exchange such commodities for corn- and wheat-based alcohol produced in western Missouri and northern Mexico distilleries. Soon thereafter these Indians became embroiled in a market economy fashioned and driven by a small but resolute cadre of entrepreneurs from Missouri, Mexico, and the upper Arkansas Valley. Eventually a much larger crowd of small-time traders joined the business of Indian alcohol and, with very few variations, emulated the tactics of the more affluent operators who preceded them.

There were more than a few Indians in the trans-Missouri West who themselves became successful alcohol traders, simply because they were legally immune from the Indian prohibition legislation dating back to the first Jefferson administration. Some of the more successful traders operated under the business model of

St. Louis entrepreneur William Bent, who initially went west for the chance to hit it big in the highly competitive Rocky Mountain fur trade but in the early 1820s eventually took advantage of the overland traffic to Taos and Santa Fe. His affection for and marriage (probably in 1837) to Owl Woman, daughter of the Southern Cheyenne leader White Thunder, was from all accounts genuine. But their union nonetheless provided Bent legal immunity to trade with Southern Cheyennes as he saw fit—including the exchange of raw alcohol for processed bison robes.

This book does not dissect Indians' drinking practices and the resulting problems. It studies how the distribution of illicit alcohol to Indians west of Missouri figured heavily in the failure of a significant aspect of federal government Indian policy: prohibition. Whatever else may have been the Indians' plight, alcoholism in the trans-Missouri West at that time was primarily a *learned behavior*, exacerbated by increasingly troubled relationships among people with little experience with alcohol and non-Indians who were veteran and often intemperate users. And an important corollary of this learned behavior is the repudiation of any notion that innate deficiencies as human beings lead Indians to excessive and abusive consumption.

The establishment of several overland routes between Missouri and New Mexico in 1821 was followed by the federal government's decision to survey one of them as a *national road* four years later, followed by the passage in 1834 of a federal law that more explicitly detailed the legal boundaries of the Indian Country. My core argument is that these events led to an increasingly unstable dynamic whereby the Osage, Kansa, Southern Cheyenne and Arapahoe,

Kiowa, and Comanche peoples, as well as several emigrant tribes east of the Mississippi whose reservations abutted or were near the overland roads, entered into an expansive and destructive trade for alcohol.

Involving huge commercial profits for the non-Indian traders by the mid-1840s, such trade would require Indians to exchange processed bison robes, government annuities, and other goods and interests for Missouri corn whiskey and Mexico wheat alcohol. One Shawnee headman would tell federal officials in 1834 that he and his people "knew the whiskey was bad." That same year the leader of another tribe whose reservation abutted the overland road to New Mexico admitted that whiskey was indeed "harmful" for his people. But, he countered, "it was the whites who first gave us whiskey [and] we did not once love it. The white man said it was good and our young men took to it. . . . We have no law and it is a difficult thing to stop. But we know it is a bad thing."[1] Such statements are representative of Indian sources who in the literature are greatly outnumbered by non-Indian sources; this is further complicated by the complexity of Indian identity.

One case in point is William Bent. In 1859—still claiming his own Southern Cheyenne Indianness through marriage—Bent was appointed federal Indian Agent for the Upper Arkansas Agency.[2] From Bent's Fort, an important facility on the road, he denounced the very kind of trade he and partners had engaged in two decades earlier. Certain questions arise: Did reports of Bent's activities in the 1830s come from Indians, whites, or others? What were the sources of reports in 1859? Should Bent himself be viewed as Indian or non-Indian? These questions are important to interpreting the historical record.

For many Indians, if not most, who lived along or near the overland roads, the white traders' promise of good times under the new dispensation was a disaster for native culture that in some ways continues into the modern era. Tribal involvement in the trade for alcohol led to internal family and band factionalism, child and female exploitation, social dysfunction and lethargy, malnutrition, and premature death. Contrary to the promises of Senator Thomas Hart Benton and his supporters in Missouri, Washington, D.C., and elsewhere—that national roads connecting Missouri with New Mexico would usher in an era of progress and prosperity for the Indians living in the so-called "intervening" Indian Country (Benton's term)—a tragically different series of events ensued. Under the federal Indian alcohol code formally introduced during the early Jefferson presidential administration and tightened up in 1847 to require large fines and incarceration for up to two years for convicted offenders, any such trade was illegal from the start. How and why the federal government—with few exceptions—failed to police and take into custody known malefactors, thereby undermining its announced program for tribal improvement, are important ancillary parts of this study. Here is less a revisionist study than one designed to fill a void in the literature regarding the overland Indian trade. It suggests also that the illegal trade in Benton's "cleared" region (i.e., between Missouri and northern New Mexico) during the second quarter of the nineteenth century may have been as important, if not more so, than the legal commerce moving between the mouth of the Kansas River and the Mexican markets far to the southwest.

In less than a half century after 1821 most Indians designated by Benton for economic and social improvement in the upper Arkansas country had been moved to the Indian territory in Oklahoma, hundreds of miles from the wagon roads to New Mexico. By then, again with support from Benton, the roads through Indian Country were rendered obsolete by a federal land-grant program subsidizing transcontinental railroad construction from the lower Mississippi Valley to the Pacific Coast, along hundreds of miles tracking the former wagon roads to Taos and Santa Fe. Not surprisingly, the deadly dealing of alcohol moved to other places—this time to Oklahoma and elsewhere.

Documentary evidence regarding the actual number of Indian people who died from alcohol consumption during the second quarter of the nineteenth century is not easy to come by. That being said, some reports of federal Indian Office officials based in or near Indian Country are more helpful and objective than often biased traveler accounts and so-called frontier newspapers. Important examples of reasonably careful reporting are those of Superintendent of Indian Affairs David D. Mitchell in the early 1840s. In 1841 he determined that at least 120 Indians residing west of Missouri had died of chronic alcohol consumption during the prior twelve months; the following year he reported that in his jurisdiction, which included most of the region traversed by the roads to Taos and Santa Fe, some 500 Indian males had died of alcohol or alcohol-related diseases in less than a year.[3]

1

Before Becknell

Within the history of U.S. territorial expansion during the first half of the eighteenth century, William Becknell of Franklin, Missouri, is renowned for skill in trading with Mexican merchants in a distant and sometimes precarious setting; for blazing new routes across Kansas, Colorado, and northern New Mexico; and for publicizing the profits to be realized from the overland trade. Some historians have characterized him as the "father" of the roads to Taos and Santa Fe. In 1821, and again in 1822, he was the first to journey along routes that other traders followed to Mexican markets more than 800 miles southwest of Franklin. A practical man, Becknell also demonstrated the value of mules over horses for drawing heavily loaded wagons across arid, often sandy terrain.[1]

George C. Sibley, head of the government's Indian trade factory at Fort Osage near modern Kansas City, apparently had met Becknell there in 1821. The celebrated Missouri trader, recalled Sibley in 1825, was simply one of those "hardy enterprising men who . . . in the true spirit of western enterprise directed [his] steps westward to the settlements of New Mexico, from whence [came] many strange and marvelous stories of inexhaustible wealth in precious metals."[2] Thus it was not just the timing of Mexican independence in 1821 and the demise of the despised Spanish tariffs, or simply being at the right place at the right time, that allowed Becknell and his companions to be ushered into a land of milk and honey. Becknell clearly knew what he was about and without hesitation, according to Sibley, went directly to the market plaza in Santa Fe.[3]

Less than a century earlier, certain individuals of more modest certitude sought to establish commercial relations between Louisiana (land drained by the Mississippi River, as claimed for France by Cavelier de La Salle in 1682) and the upper Rio Grande country claimed by Spain. Possibly the most dedicated of these were the brothers Pierre and Paul Mallet, who with the blessing of French Louisiana governor Jean-Baptiste LaMoune de Bienville set out from Illinois country in 1739 with seven men to determine if the Missouri River would eventually lead to the Spanish settlements in and around Santa Fe. According to traditional accounts, the Mallet party ascended the Missouri to the Arikara country of present central South Dakota, but more recent research has them traveling not far beyond the mouth of the Platte River, up the south fork of that river to the Front Range of the Rockies, south along that range to Taos by way of the Raton Pass utilized by William Becknell's party in 1821, and then on to Santa Fe.[4]

The Missouri River obviously did not lead to the upper Rio Grande, but this disappointment was lessened by the guarded welcome extended the Mallet party members, who were allowed to remain in Santa Fe or return home. The Mallet brothers and two others opted to return to New Orleans, in part by way of the Canadian and Mississippi Rivers; two chose to remain in Santa Fe, and the remaining three traveled back to Illinois country. Governor Bienville was impressed to the degree that in 1741 he authorized a large commercial expedition to Santa Fe, this time to travel by boats on the Canadian River, commanded by Fabry de la Bruyère. But after receiving advice from some Osage hunters some 80 miles southeast of present Oklahoma City that it was impossible to navigate the Canadian all the way to Santa Fe, La Bruyère and his crew gave up and turned back. The venture, which cost the French crown 22,600 livre, was a disappointment for French officials in New Orleans.[5] But their appetite for commerce with Santa Fe had been whetted, and by no means did news of La Bruyère's failure squash all French efforts to open up trade there. The fatal blow was the French and Indian War in 1756; the 1763 Treaty of Paris ended that war and virtually expelled the French from North America.

Even so, a number of Frenchmen continued to search out or actually visit Santa Fe. In 1748 some Jicarilla visitors at Taos told resident missionary Fray Antonio that thirty-three French traders had visited their village east of Taos. The following year three Frenchmen, with some Comanche traders, were reported at the Taos fair. Pierre Mallet and four companions returned to the upper Rio Grande in 1750 but were arrested at Pecos, and in 1752 two more Frenchmen were arrested and had their trade goods confiscated by Spanish authorities in Santa Fe. And as late as 1806 or early 1807, Manuel Lisa (or some employees of his St. Louis Missouri Fur Company) made it all the way from St. Louis to Santa Fe. Lisa had been awarded a federal license to trade with the Osages in 1806 and was known to have used alcohol as a trade item; the actual merchandise and other details of his journey to Santa Fe, hundreds of miles west of the Osages, are uncertain.[6]

Concerned that the buffer lands of Louisiana that had shielded their estates, missions, and mines for well over a century were in danger of being overrun, Spanish officials resorted to more restrictive tariffs and other regulations to ward off foreigners. In fact, the matter became of greater concern after ownership of most of Louisiana, with the sweep of a pen, was transferred from France to Spain by the secret Treaty of Fontainebleau in 1762. Even so, traders with little awareness or concern regarding European politics and diplomacy continued to knock on the gates at Santa Fe. By the time Napoleon sold Louisiana to the United States, in 1803, the "profane and aggressive Anglo-Saxons"—as one historian of exploration and empire described them—were eager and ready to lead the charge.[7] They knew only too well how slow and expensive it was for residents of the upper Rio Grande to be supplied with cottons, silks, blankets, leather goods, hardware, foodstuffs, spices, and other consumer goods from distant Mexico City and Veracruz.

In 1804 William Morrison of Kaskaskia, Illinois, outfitted Jeannot Metoyer and Baptiste Lalande for a business expedition to Santa Fe; Spanish documents note their presence in Santa Fe the following year but are unclear regarding actual transactions. The same records tell of a Lorenzo Durocher who came down to New Mexico and Santa Fe from the upper Missouri Indian Country in 1805. Other arrivals a year later were St. Louis fur traders Jean la Croix and André Terien, as well as the businessman James Purcell of Baird's Town, Kentucky. Like the experiences of Morrison's men, the details of these visitations to Santa Fe are unknown. Less uncertain are the experiences in Santa Fe, in 1812, of Robert McKnight, James Baird, Michael McDonough, Samuel Chambers, and perhaps as many as four other Missourians. They were arrested as spies, their goods were commandeered by Spanish officials, and most (perhaps all) were incarcerated in a Chihuahua prison until

Mexican independence nine years later led to their release. More evidence that Spanish authorities, in the decade preceding Becknell's journey to Santa Fe, were tightening up on foreign traders working their craft among their own people was the arrest of Auguste Chouteau and Jules de Mun, in the spring of 1817, in the upper Arkansas Basin somewhere west of present Pueblo, Colorado. Like Manuel Lisa a decade earlier, Chouteau and de Mun could produce an official trade license issued by the U.S. government authorizing them to engage in trade with "Arapahoes, Comanches, etc." in that area. But all that got them was 48 hours in a Santa Fe prison and the confiscation of $30,000 worth of furs and other personal property. Three years later another trader, David Meriwether, was arrested and jailed in Santa Fe.[8]

By contrast, this was not the experience of people attending native trade fairs during the pre-Becknell period. Beginning in the late 1750s, Taos was a place where Indians, Spaniards, and trappers of mostly obscure nationality met annually to exchange goods. Pueblo villagers, Eastern Apaches, Plains Caddoans, and Southern Sioux traded hides, minerals, pelts, and preserved meat for beads, knives, calico, tobacco, guns, and horses. Smaller but no less noteworthy were trade fairs more sporadically convened in nearby Picuris and Pecos, as well as other, less permanent locations on plains to the east. Some of these fairs continued until the closing years of the eighteenth century, and as late as 1821—the year Becknell made his first trip to New Mexico—Western Comanches hosted a large trade fair at the Big Timbers groves along the Arkansas River in present Prowers County, Colorado. In addition to the host Comanche peoples, some 500 Kiowa, Apache, Shoshone, Cheyenne, and Arapaho households took part in the fair.[9] But unlike Lisa, Chouteau, Baird, and other Americans only a few years earlier, no Indians at Big Timbers were arrested and hauled off to a New Mexico jail. Nor were some of the very same Indians who for decades had been engaged in trade with the "Comanchero" merchants of Santa Fe.[10]

By the beginning of the nineteenth century most American and Indian traders were viewed with suspicion by Spanish officials as to what such dealings might mean for the future of Spain's northernmost province. Would an increased flow of American trade goods provide the solution to the long-standing economic imbalance between the undersupplied region surrounding Taos and Santa Fe and the more prosperous provinces to the south? Would less restrictive trade regulations provide the setting for a negotiated annexation or outright military seizure of the region by the United States? Certainly it was apparent that the arrest (and unexpected release soon thereafter) of an American military officer, Lieutenant Zebulon Montgomery Pike, on Spanish soil near the confluence of the Rio Conejos and Rio Grande, in February 1807, did not improve relations between Americans and Spain's colonial officials.[11] Ultimately, however, it was Mexican independence from Spain that allowed officials in New Mexico to liberalize the Spanish trade code and thereby welcome traders like William Becknell to inland ports of call like Taos and Santa Fe.

For Becknell timing was everything. The Mexican independence movement began in central Mexico nearly two decades before Becknell embarked on his venture, which he himself claimed was "for the purpose of trading for Horses and Mules, and catching Wild Animals of every description." Becknell and his five companions left Arrow Rock near Franklin, Missouri, on September 1, 1821. Three months earlier, on May 24, representatives of the Spanish crown and the Mexican revolutionary leader Colonel Augustín de

Iturbide signed the Treaty of Cordoba, ending the eleven-year revolution and recognizing Mexican independence. On September 24, Becknell and his men reached the Arkansas; on October 21 they followed a left fork of the Arkansas (most likely the Purgatoire River near present Las Animas, Colorado), then crossed over to the upper Canadian River south of present Springer, New Mexico. By mid-November, at Puertocito near present Las Vegas, New Mexico, they were intercepted by a Mexican military detachment commanded by Captain Pedro Ignacio Gallego, who advised them of Mexico's independence and then escorted them to Santa Fe via San Miguel. At the provincial capital they were greeted with kindness and respect by Governor Facundo Melgares and, in the words of Becknell, "with apparent joy and pleasure." They easily disposed of their goods at a profit, accompanied by requests to return with more goods of equal quality from the United States. By mid-December 1821, Becknell and his companions were back in Missouri, busily planning a return trip.[12]

Thus the year 1821 is viewed by western historians as momentous in the history of overland commerce to northern New Mexico. Other events that same year confirm this. On February 22, 1821, for example, the Adams-Onís Transcontinental Treaty negotiated in Washington two years earlier, by John Quincy Adams of the United States and Don Luis de Onis of Spain, was formally entered in force. The paramount stipulation of the treaty was Spain's agreement to relinquish all claims to eastern and western Florida in return for U.S. recognition of Spanish sovereignty over Texas, California, and the intervening territory of present New Mexico, Arizona, and parts of Utah, Colorado, and Wyoming. More specifically, in Article 3 it set the boundary between the United States and Spain, west of the 100th Meridian, along the southern bank of the

Arkansas River west to its source in the Rocky Mountains, north to the 42nd Parallel, and west to the Pacific Coast—part of the area Becknell and his men crossed on their way to Santa Fe less than a year later.[13] As well, it was the area where major problems between the Plains Indians, the Taos and Santa Fe traders, and the federal government became manifest soon after 1821.

In 1821 Thomas Hart Benton was elected as one of Missouri's first federal senators. Native of North Carolina, frontier lawyer, admirer of Thomas Jefferson, former aide-de-camp to General Andrew Jackson, lieutenant colonel of the Thirty-ninth U.S. Infantry during the War of 1812, caustic St. Louis newspaper editor, and champion of southern culture and values, Senator Benton in Washington was selected to be chairman of the Committee on Indian Affairs and member of the Committee on Military Affairs. It was from these positions that the so-called Magnificent Missourian exerted remarkable influence and power over the roads to Taos and Santa Fe.[14]

Perhaps most important of all was evidence that 1821 would be the last year for a network of U.S. government–operated Indian trading posts (the *factory system*). One of the most important of these posts was Fort Osage in western Missouri, where Becknell stopped en route to the western Plains and Santa Fe. From the time of their establishment in 1796 these factories were vigorously opposed by the large fur companies and later by most private traders planning to compete with Becknell in Taos and Santa Fe. The final amendment to the bill abolishing these factories was submitted by Benton, who insisted that the government trade houses dating back to the second Washington administration were "worse than useless." Four days later, on March 19, 1822, the bill passed without debate, and the road to New Mexico became much more inviting.[15]

2

"Vacant" Land

When Becknell left the mouth of the Kansas River west of Franklin he had no major east-to-west river to guide him until he arrived at the Great Bend of the Arkansas River, some 200 miles southwest of modern Kansas City. Traveling along the Arkansas another 100 miles southwest brought Becknell to the very heart of the Great American Desert, so named by Lieutenant Zebulon M. Pike in 1810 based on his observations four years earlier while searching (unsuccessfully, as it turned out) for the headwaters of the Arkansas. In 1820 Major Stephen H. Long confirmed this region to be an inhospitable wilderness while on an expedition to the upper Platte and Arkansas Basins.

Pike's description of the area bisected by the Arkansas and Platte Rivers was more detailed regarding the arid climate and other environmental features detrimental to farming, but Long's 1821 map—with the words "GREAT AMERICAN DESERT" prominently displayed across the High Plains west of the 100th Meridian—was a more powerful deterrent for Americans hoping to begin a new and productive life there. Not surprisingly, then, and with outright disregard for thousands of Indians who had hunted and traded on those same plains for centuries, one New York newspaperman insisted, in 1859, that the Great Plains were "nearly destitute of human beings" and that the "Desert" was actually expanding.[1]

Even so, the reports of Pike and Long presented no insurmountable obstacles to Senator Benton and his supporters regarding the possibility of settling the region. For one thing, most of the area east of the Great Bend, as Benton surely knew but apparently believed was more important for others to articulate openly, was no desert at all. In fact, west of Missouri to the 97th Meridian—roughly half the distance to the Great Bend—possessed a climate and topography not much different from those in western Missouri. Climate research bears this out. Nineteenth- and early-twentieth-century precipitation records over thirty-year intervals, for example, indicate that the annual rainfall at the mouth of the Kansas River (38 inches) was more than twice that at the western border of modern Kansas (16 inches), leading to the classification of the western one-fourth of Kansas (including all of the area traveled by Becknell) as a "middle latitude semiarid zone"; and the remaining part of Kansas (also traversed by Becknell) as a "humid continental zone," with low to high relative humidity averages well in line with the rainfall averages of the two zones.[2]

Southwest of Kansas, along Becknell's original route through the Oklahoma Panhandle, and on through southeastern Colorado and northeastern New Mexico, the semiarid zone continued until rendered more humid by the Sangre de Cristo elevation, where Taos and Santa Fe were located. In short, white settlement for a few hundred miles west of Missouri was possible, perhaps desirable for whites and even for a limited number of emigrant Indians from the east. In a letter to Senator Benton in 1825, Franklin resident and veteran Santa Fe trader August Storrs reported that the area west of Missouri to the Great Bend was "admirably fitted to such a purpose" and that in fact it was "among the most beautiful and fertile tracts of country" he had ever seen. Storrs continued:

> Streams, lined with timber, intersect and beautify it in every direction. There are delightful landscapes, over which Flora has scattered here beauties with a wanton hand, and upon whose bosom innumerable wild animals display their amazing numbers. . . . As I passed through that delightful region, I could not help regretting that it should be a waste of nature, and felt a secret assurance that, at some future period, flocks would feed upon it abundant herbage, and numerous population would derive support from its fertility.[3]

Beyond that, however, it was only arid and "vacant" land and, according to Storrs, similar to what Arkansas resident Albert Pike in the fall of 1831 described thus in his journal while heading to Santa Fe by way of the Lower Cimarron Spring,[4] 60 miles southwest of present Cimarron, Kansas:

> After following the Arkansas, about eighty miles [beyond the Great Bend], we forded it with our wagons. . . . [B]etween the Arkansas and Semaron [Cimarron] . . . [it] was not level but rather composed of immense undulations, as though it had once been the bed of a tumultuous ocean—a hard, dry surface of fine gravel, incapable, almost, of supporting vegetation. The general features of this whole desert—its

> sterility, dryness, and unconquerable barrenness—are the same wherever I have been in it.[5]

Clearly, according to Pike, it was an "empty wilderness" encompassing more than half the country between western Missouri and northern New Mexico—certainly not the kind of virgin land to excite an expansionist politician such as Benton.

Especially questionable for Albert Pike, accustomed as he and his companions were to wood or stone houses, well-planned farm plots, cash crops, fenced pastures, and domestic livestock in their native Arkansas, was whether anyone could establish and sustain a viable settlement anywhere near Lower Cimarron Spring or, for that matter, at any point in the adjacent and no less dreary region from the upper Platte drainage down to the Canadian/Red River country more than 400 miles south.

If the answer was no—as surely it was—then it was qualified to some extent by Pike himself in his report of 1831. As the number of oxen decreased, he wrote, there was an increase in the number of wolves following the wagons, eager to feast on the faltering animals. But this did not keep him from grumbling more about the loss of fresh breakfast meat to wolves than of wolves stalking and devouring fallen oxen who were his essential means of traveling to Santa Fe. Said Pike:

> I can give the reader some idea of their [the wolves'] number and voracity, by informing him, that one night, just at sunset, we killed six buffaloes [more properly, bison] and having time to butcher and take to camp only three, we left the other three on the ground, skinned and in part cut up. The next

> morning there was not a hide, a bone, or a bit of meat, within fifty yards of the place.[6]

Thus while Pike's casual and almost routine reporting of the bison incident was presented as less newsworthy than dying oxen and the gluttony of wolves, it did point to the vital role of bison in the human occupation—indeed, survival—on the Great Plains.

Precisely how many bison at one time grazed the short-grass prairie may never be known. Some estimates have the peak number at about 25 million animals, with a mid-nineteenth century estimate for the southern herd (south of the Platte River) between 6 million and 7 million, and perhaps many millions more.[7] The point here is that there were people living in the country Pike dismissed as an "unconquerable wilderness," people whose ancestors had been on the semiarid plains centuries prior to Becknell's journey in 1821. They, too, were hunters—but more dependent on bison protein and fat, and other nonedible bison products, than Pike and his overland followers could ever have imagined. They were a resourceful people but at a difficult time in their lives.[8] Not surprisingly, then, the death of Jedediah Smith at the hands of the Comanches in 1831, or the killing of E. S. Minter by the Pawnees that same year, indicated that not all Indian hunters were receptive to the bison trade that allowed one company alone to ship 15,000 processed robes over the Santa Fe road to warehouses in Westport and St. Louis.[9]

An exploratory trip taken by U.S. Factor (or government trader) George C. Sibley in 1811 to Indian Country between the mouth of the Kansas and the Great Bend of the Arkansas and south to present Oklahoma added force to the argument against a "vacant" wilderness west of Missouri. Anticipating August Storrs's intelligence more than a decade later, Sibley's 1811 report to Indian Agent William Clark[10] called attention to some native settlements so attractive they might appeal to even the most discerning white residents of Missouri, perhaps to those in other border states as well. A large Kansa village some 35 miles south of where the Santa Fe road would soon head southwest from Council Grove, in present Morris County, Kansas, was established "in a charming elevated prairie" surrounded by "a fine tract of country." To the north, on a bank of the Loup branch of the Platte River, a Pawnee village was sensibly positioned "on a beautiful level prairie." And across the present Kansas-Oklahoma border southeast of the Great Bend, the Osage chief White Hair's large village was surrounded with game "of all kinds," soil that was "fertile and fruitful," and a climate "salubrious and pleasant."[11] Thus while Sibley conceded that the area east of the Great Bend to the western Missouri border, and extending north and south of the Arkansas for hundreds of miles, was attractive and at least *partially* settled by Indians, the overriding implication was that here was an ideal place for *non-Indian* settlement as well—what Sibley later described as a natural extension of the "Garden of Missouri,"[12] an extension that would become even more productive by an overland road connecting thriving fields with riverboats churning down the Missouri toward the markets of St. Louis and beyond.

In this context it is important to remember that discussion regarding the removal of eastern Indians to the trans-Mississippi West began almost as soon as the Louisiana Purchase Treaty was signed (April 30, 1803). The first general removal statute was signed by President Jackson on May 26, 1830, but as early as August 11, 1803, President Thomas Jefferson brought up the matter in a letter to Senator John Breckenridge of Kentucky. Contrary to the belief that Indian removal had the virtue of discouraging white settlement in upper Louisiana, Jefferson told Breckenridge that a better use for the region would be to provide "establishments" for Indians east of the Mississippi in exchange for their own country, followed by the opening of land offices leading to white settlement (mostly explorers, traders, miners, the military, and government agents for cultivating commerce with the Indians), and eventually a "range of states" west of the Mississippi.[13] It was a thoughtful suggestion and possibly one that Senator Benton himself might have endorsed had he been in the Senate in 1803.

But he was not. Nearly two decades later, with little more accurate information than Jefferson had in 1803 regarding how many native people actually lived on the land where eastern Indians might be relocated, the War Department selected Reverend Josiah Morse to count Indians throughout the United States, including the region "between the Missouri and Arkansas rivers & between the Mississippi and Rocky Mountains." It was a region equal in size to nearly the entire United States east of the Appalachians, but Morse counted only 101,072 natives for the entire region.[14] Given that the Comanches alone numbered some 40,000 before the smallpox epidemics of the 1780s devastated them,[15] and that the "high plains population rose steeply in the late eighteenth century, then climbed more sharply after 1800,"[16] Reverend Morse's low numbers may have comforted the War Department and those who believed in a no-man's-land beyond the Great Bend. But sentiment of this sort ignored reality.

Beginning in the late seventeenth century, or perhaps as part of an earlier movement away from the western Great Lakes, northwestern Minnesota, the Montana mountains, and southwestern

Wyoming, thousands of people whose group designations were (or soon would be) Western Sioux, Arapahoes, Cheyennes, Kiowas, Comanches, and others migrated or were forced by other native groups to new locations such as the Yellowstone Valley, the Dakota Black Hills, the valleys of the central Rocky Mountains, and eventually to the central Great Plains, from the Arkansas and its southern tributaries to the Platte and its drainage from the north.[17] En route some groups transformed their economies from a mix of horticulture and hunting to hunting and trading as their primary means of survival. By the time Becknell crossed the Plains in 1821, these tribes were well situated there and, in varying degrees, had guns and horses and had at least tasted alcohol, primarily from British and American fur traders to the north[18] and the French to the south and east. Their aggregate number alone was easily more than 70 percent of the total for the trans-Mississippi West that Morse had reported to the War Department.

While Indians from the northern prairie-plains and mountains were firming up their spheres of occupation on the south-central Plains, the federal government was moving irrevocably toward a comprehensive plan for Indian removal, one that could be applied to any tribe occupying land east of the Mississippi River. This was achieved on May 26, 1830, when President Andrew Jackson signed "an Act to provide for an exchange of lands with the Indians residing in any of the states or territories, and their removal west of the river Mississippi."[19] Although some of the more negative results of this law as applied to the region only recently traveled by Becknell may have been anticipated by the law's authors, only twenty-three words (italicized below) of the near 600 total for the 1830 law actually dealt with the millions of acres of western land in question:

> It shall be lawful for the President of the United States to cause so much of any territory belonging to the United States, *west of the river Mississippi, not included in any other state or organized territory, and to which the Indian title has been extinguished* [emphasis added], as he may judge necessary, to be divided into a suitable number of districts, for the reception of such tribes or nations of Indians as may choose to exchange the lands where they now reside, and remove there.[20]

Precisely what the phrase "Indian title" in the 1830 law meant was uncertain because the U.S. Supreme Court had ruled in 1823 that Indians held no legal title to their lands and therefore could not legally convey titles to others. Possibly anticipating similar or other problems related to Indian land and removal, the War Department—charged with administering and executing federal Indian policy—determined in 1825 to pursue a series of so-called friendship treaties with those Plains tribes willing to talk about trade regulations, non-Indian travel across their lands, foreigners, and related diplomatic matters.

Selected to head the mission, which by its very authorization was an overt rejection of Pike's and Long's negative accounting of the country west of the Great Bend, was Brigadier General Henry Atkinson, who during 1819–1820 had commanded an expedition organized to fortify the middle and upper Missouri country, including the construction of a military post at the mouth of the Yellowstone. But that expedition fell victim to cuts in War Department funding and related logistical problems, resulting in Atkinson going no farther up the Missouri than Council Bluffs (near modern Omaha), where his men constructed Fort Missouri (later renamed

Fort Atkinson) and where he met with members of several Pawnee bands whom he chided for stealing guns and horses from one of his subordinates.[21]

From the War Department's perspective the Yellowstone Expedition of 1825 was more successful. General Atkinson, with the assistance of the Upper Missouri Indian Agent Benjamin O'Fallon, participated in the whirlwind execution of friendship treaties with more that a dozen tribes (or bands) at Fort Atkinson and points up the Missouri River as far northwest as the mouth of the Yellowstone from the late spring to the early fall of 1825. Those tribes who agreed to be friends with the United States and, more important, to allow legally authorized U.S. citizens to travel across their lands included the Poncas, Otoes, Missourias, Mahas (Omahas), Teton Sioux, Oglala Sioux (and related Sioux bands), Cheyennes, Crows, Arikaras, Mandans, and several bands of Pawnees.[22] Clearly, the road to Santa Fe was prompting War Department concerns for the safe passage of overland travelers and traders, even though some of the 1825 treaties were with tribes whose principal villages and principal hunting grounds were hundreds of miles north.

Some of the 1825 treaties, however, were more explicit regarding the reported dangers of traveling from western Missouri to Taos and Santa Fe. In treaties with the Pawnees, Cheyennes, Crows, and the Sioune and Oglala Sioux, no real negotiations took place, as most of the actual wording of the treaties had been prepared by General Atkinson and Agent O'Fallon well in advance of their travel up the Missouri. The rest was relatively simple: Following a liberal distribution of blankets, strouding, guns, knives, tobacco, coffee, sugar, and sundry trinkets, Atkinson's and O'Fallon's paramount role was to persuade the most distinguished chiefs and warriors of the five tribes to place their marks at the appropriate line of the treaty document, thereby agreeing "whilst on their distant excursions, [not to] molest or interrupt any American citizens or citizens who may be passing from the United States to New Mexico, or returning thence to the United States." The Cheyenne Treaty was concluded at the mouth of the Teton (Bad) River, nearly 400 miles north of the Great Bend of the Arkansas, and the Crows met the treaty delegation at the Mandan villages, 150 miles farther north.[23] Truly, the Great Father in Washington was concerned for the safety of its white citizens on the remote but increasingly popular road between western Missouri and Santa Fe.

In 1825 Atkinson and O'Fallon were not the only officials concluding treaties regarding Indian-white relations along the Santa Fe road. That year the first formal negotiations for Indian removal to the area immediately west of Missouri took place in St. Louis. Here Superintendant William Clark met with leaders of the "Shawnee Indians residing with the State of Missouri" concerning their removal from a 25-square-mile reservation "near Cape Geredeau" [*sic*] in southeastern Missouri, to a 50-square-mile tract in the southeastern corner of present Kansas, well over 100 miles south of Becknell's route to New Mexico in 1821. But the all-important Article 3 of the 1825 treaty stated that if the Shawnees were dissatisfied with the location of this tract they could make this known to Clark, who "in lieu thereof [would] assign to them an equal quantity of land, to be selected on the Kansas River, and laid off either south or north of that river, and west of the boundary of Missouri, *not reserved or ceded to any other tribe*" [emphasis added].[24]

The Shawnees took advantage of Article 3 and selected a tract directly south of the Kansas River extending 30 miles west of the Missouri state line,[25] which placed them along both sides of Becknell's route for the entire 30 miles on land that, according to the 1825 treaty, was theretofore vacant (i.e., "not reserved or ceded to any other tribe"). And unlike the Atkinson and O'Fallon treaties of that same year, the Shawnees did not grant permission for non-Indian travel across their new reservation; neither did they promise to refrain form molesting or interrupting any American citizens traveling to and from New Mexico, as had been specifically required of the Pawnees, Cheyennes, Crows, and two groups of Sioux.

Certainly, increasing commercial traffic across the entire width of their Kansas River reservation would have a dramatic impact on Shawnee life. According to figures compiled by Josiah Gregg, a veteran Santa Fe trader, the cost of goods in the United States shipped to Santa Fe and Chihuahua on the overland road in 1825 was $65,000, carried in thirty-seven wagons; in 1826 it had increased to $90,000, carried in sixty wagons. Five years later the cost of goods had increased to $250,000, carried in 130 wagons.[26] In addition to the obvious demand for consumer goods in the upper Rio Grande and Chihuahua markets to the south, such economic data were reflective of an important aspect of Missouri's booming frontier economy, one that, alongside agriculture, included overland trade as well. Population growth bears this out. Howard County, home of Arrow Rock, from whence Becknell started his trek to Santa Fe in 1821, had a population of 12,000 in 1820. Land advertised at the local Booneslick land office was then selling for $4 per acre, compared to $2.84 per acre at St. Louis, 150 miles east. One year later, the population of Howard County had increased to 13,427, which made it the fastest-growing county of the fifteen counties then in Missouri.[27]

In the meantime, new commercial activity materialized on the eastern and western perimeters of the overland road. In 1827, Lexington merchant James Aull opened a branch store in Independence, near the eastern terminus of the Santa Fe road. To compensate for a poor corn crop in the area that year, Aull diversified his mercantile operations by ordering twenty-four barrels of rye whiskey from an eastern wholesaler—exclusively, it was reported, "for the Santa Fe trade."[28] Also in 1827, James Hyatt McGee came to western Missouri with a government contract to provide flour for the removal Shawnees and soon thereafter constructed a distillery near Westport "as an adjunct to his grist mill" located only a few miles from the Santa Fe road.[29] And more than 700 miles to the southwest, during the winter of 1827–1828, Matthew Kinkead, Samuel Chambers, and William Workman erected the first large-yield wheat distillery in Taos, approximately 3 miles up the Little Rio Grande from Ranchos.[30] Competitors to these pioneers in the alcohol trade would soon appear, in both western Missouri and northern New Mexico. The stage was thus set for significant economic growth and profits in an increasingly more populated land.

3

Cleared Land

An eminent historian of federal Indian policy has concluded that "Indian treaties, when all is said and done, were a political anomaly." That is, the generally recognized rule of a treaty being a formal agreement between two or more sovereign nations, when applied to the 367 ratified treaties between the United States and those Indian tribes formerly recognized by the United States prior to the termination of the Indian treaty process in 1871, was the exception, not the rule. With this in mind, it would be difficult to find a more striking anomaly than the state of Indian affairs at the confluence of the Missouri and Kansas Rivers, not far from where Becknell, in 1821, entered an unsettled region that most Americans at the time, including high-ranking officials in government, called "Indian Country."

Words referring to or describing such a land had no legal stature (certainly not from the government's point of view) unless by treaty an Indian nation had signed off on where its lands actually were—and, conversely, where they were not. Directly west of Missouri were more than 800,000 square miles purchased by the United States from France, with vague or unreliable data regarding where the southern and western borders were, let alone the number and cultural diversity of the natives living there. Here also was a place deficient of effective U.S. judicial authority prior to 1834, certainly when compared to Missouri and the states east of the Mississippi. And here also were numerous indigenous peoples who by Becknell's time were increasingly concerned over the invasion of their traditional domains by non-Indian travelers, traders, and commercial hunters. It was a disquieting situation, one involving some 15,000 Southern (Village) Sioux, including the Chiwere-speaking Otoes and Missourias, as well as the Dhegiha-speaking Quapaws, Poncas, Omahas, Osages, and Kansas. The 6,000 Osage members then residing in present western Missouri along the river bearing their name (and in a few satellite villages in present northeastern Oklahoma), and some 1,600 Kansas in present northeastern Kansas,[1] were belligerent and often outright hostile to non-Indians seeking to hunt and trade along the route Becknell had traveled from Arrow Rock to the Great Bend of the Arkansas in 1821 and beyond.

Having migrated westward from the lower Ohio Valley or (according to some sources) from as far east as the Virginia Piedmont or the Carolinas, the Dhegian-Sioux were well entrenched in the lower Missouri Valley by no later than 1673, based on Father Jacques Marquette's map of his voyage down the Mississippi that year.[2] These tribes lived by a combination of garden farming and biannual hunting expeditions, with a small but growing trade, especially in guns, ammunition, and alcohol, with Euro-Americans. They cultivated beans, maize, sunflowers, and squash near their core villages, and in the summer and winter seasons they hunted bison, deer, and elk, with entire bands or villages moving to the western prairie-plains to find the animals, sometimes as far west as the present Kansas-Colorado border. In so doing, the precise boundaries of the Osage and Kansa domains directly west of the mouth of the Missouri in 1821 were anything but certain, a recurring problem for non-Indians seeking to establish safe and unobstructed trails west of Missouri. And not far north of Becknell's route across present central Kansas were the Pawnees, a Caddoan-speaking people opposed to the Kansa and Osage hunters harvesting increasingly valuable bison robes in what they (the Pawnees) viewed as their exclusive country. And only a few miles directly west of the present eastern Kansas border were the Missouri Shawnees, as well as other removal tribes soon to arrive from the east—all of whom, of course, were anything but welcome to the "indigenous" Osages, Kansas, and Pawnees.

Providing some tentative intelligence regarding the boundaries of these sundry Indian nations in the lower Missouri and Kansas Basins was a map prepared by the St. Louis surveyor René Paul in 1816 titled "A Map Exhibiting the Territorial Limits of several Nations & Tribes agreeable to the Notes of A. Chouteau."[3] Paul was the son-in-law of Auguste Chouteau, a prominent St. Louis businessman and civic leader who had served with the territorial governors of Missouri (William Clark) and Illinois (Ninian Edwards) on a federal commission that had negotiated the Portage de Sioux Peace and Friendship Treaty with the Osages in 1815. With his brother Pierre, Auguste had been involved in the upper Missouri fur trade since the early 1780s and was widely recognized as an authority on native history, ethnography, geography, and especially land matters in the trans-Mississippi West. He also was well connected with War Department and Indian Office officials in Washington, and it was his notes that Paul credited as the principal sources for his 1816 map. Significantly, Paul's map displayed no vacant terrain between the Osage and Kansa domains over which Becknell's party would travel to New Mexico five years later.[4] According to Paul and Chouteau, Becknell's 1821 route to Santa Fe intruded onto Osage and Kansa land from the very start.

In this context it should be noted that in 1808 the Great and Little Osage, in a high-handed treaty written by War Department officials in Washington and placed into effect by the Missouri territorial governor Meriwether Lewis, were chided for their hostility toward neighboring tribes and for plundering white settlements in western Missouri. The terms of the treaty were specific. For a blacksmith, a grist mill, and a renewable $1,500 annuity, the carrot for the Osages was a trade factory (the future Fort Osage) designed primarily for their own benefit, leading toward their becoming "more closely under the protection of the United States than they had been before." For such paltry consideration the Osages ceded all lands south of the Missouri River and east of a north-south line along the eastern boundary of the Fort Osage factory grounds, down to the Arkansas River hundreds of miles south—an immense extent of land. Negotiations were short and to the point, a classic example of treatymaking. The Osage leaders who signed the treaty were given certificates to trade at the new Fort Osage; those who did not were denied any goods, "either from the factory or from private traders, under any pretext whatsoever."[5]

The Special United States Commissioner for the Osage Treaty was Pierre Chouteau, licensed trader and Indian Office agent for the Osages, who certified that the Arrow Rock to Fort Osage portion of Becknell's 1821 New Mexico journey as ceded was "unobstructed" or "unsettled" government land. But beyond Fort Osage it was not. Here the problem was the Kansas, who, unlike the supposedly placated Osages, were determined to hold the line and block any overland travel west of Fort Osage. In fact their obstructionism was so determined that by October 1808, less than a month prior to the Osages' submission to Chouteau at Fort Osage, government factor Sibley was "induced to shut the store [at Fort Osage] against them [the Kansa] on account of their solent and violent conduct."[6] This was no aberration. In fact, for decades the Kansas had been stealing and terrorizing Indians and non-Indians, from the mouth of the Kansas River to the upper Arkansas and Smoky Hill Basins in present eastern Colorado. One member of a fur-trading expedition to the Mandan and Gros Ventre villages in the late spring of 1809 wrote:

> The Cansas [Kansas] have long been the terror of the neighboring Indians, their temerity is hardly credible; a few weeks ago since a band of 100 [Kansa] warriors entered the Pauni [Pawnee] village, or what is generally called the Paunies [Pawnee] Republic, and killed the principal chief and his family of 15 souls. . . . These people cannot be at peace with the white or red people; they rob, murder and destroy when opportunity offers.[7]

Kansa difficulties with the Otoes to the northeast and the continued advance of white settlers into the area east of Fort Osage led to Governor Clark's instructions to Sibley in 1818 to "enter into a provisional arrangement"[8] with the Kansas for the purchase of a portion of their lands in present Jackson, Cass, Lafayette, and Johnson Counties in Missouri, as well as a large area west of the mouth of the Kansas River extending to the upper Neosho Basin near the future Santa Fe road outfitting post at Council Grove.

Sibley soon worked out an agreement providing that the Kansas, in exchange for the land cessions sought by Clark, were to receive the services of a blacksmith and be paid $2,000 worth of cloth, vermilion, guns, ammunition, kettles, hoes, axes, flint, awls, and tobacco each September for an indefinite term.[9] It was a bargain for the government, explained Sibley, who bragged that one 20-square-mile tract alone in the ceded territory would, within two years, be equal in value to ten years of annual payments to the Kansas.[10] But the agreement was turned down by the Indian Office for reasons not publicly announced but widely believed to be the white settlers' demands to Senator Benton for an even larger cession from the Kansa—plus more land from the Osages as well.

As greater numbers of hunters and traders ventured into the region west of Missouri and Arkansas Territory, thereby creating the need for roads like those still being used on former Indian lands in the east, and as political pressure in Washington mounted in support of a more general removal policy for tribes east of the Mississippi River, requiring millions of acres of newly ceded land, it was apparent that specifics were needed regarding the actual boundaries of the Osages, Kansas, and Pawnees—to name only a few Indian nations in the trans-Missouri West that might be adversely affected. Of particular interest were roads similar to the one Becknell had traveled in 1821. Would the government allow free and unobstructed passage over these native lands in the West? The all-important Article 3 of the 1802 Indian Trade and Intercourse Act stated that anyone who "cross[ed] over" an Indian boundary listed in any treaty but without an official government passport should "forfeit a sum not exceeding a hundred dollars, or be imprisoned not exceeding six months." The same law, with regard to an undisguised pork-barrel road across Indian property, from the

Washington district to the Mero district in east-central Tennessee, held that the president of the United States could, under authority of the 1802 Act, prohibit all non-Indian travel simply if Indian signators objected.[11] Could this happen on the much longer and more dangerous road from Missouri to Santa Fe?

In St. Louis, Governor Clark became concerned and turned to Sibley for advice. In 1811, it will be recalled,[12] Sibley, the ever-busy resident of western Missouri, had traveled widely in the Smoky Hill, upper Arkansas, and northern Canadian River country. He was a veteran head of the Fort Osage factory, one of the most successful factories in the entire country, and a seasoned Indian Office functionary who had dealt with numerous Indians and their problems for more than a decade. In short, what Sibley said about Indians west of Missouri in the early nineteenth century mattered. His response to Clark came in 1819, in a letter worth recounting in its entirety for its insight and candor on the problem of tribal landownership in the trans-Missouri West:

> The Claims of our Indian Tribes to lands are so extremely vague and undefined, so conflicting and intermixed; that I cannot conceive a much more difficult task than to assign to each Tribe its proper limits—Therefore I think it would much better comport with the liberal views and benevolent policy of our government toward those poor creatures, to satisfy them all by annuities, in proportion to their numbers, *for such lands as we desire to add to our domain* [emphasis added]. . . . Perhaps it would be just to say, that the forest and wilds of the Missouri [basin] belong in common to those Nations of Indians who live contiguous to them and Hunt thro' them. And when our Govt thinks proper to reclaim

> those wilds for the use of our People, remuneration ought to be made in common to those Tribes whose natural pursuits are thus interfered with—Thus we should do justice to all, and satisfy all; which you know is the precise object of Govt; and which I am very certain can never be attained in any other manner.[13]

Little wonder, then, that Sibley heaped praise on Becknell for his overland trade expedition across some of the very land Sibley's proposal contemplated clearing of Indian title. "I believe the honour of the first enterprise of this sort belongs to William Becknell," wrote Sibley in 1824. Becknell's outfit consisted of only a few hundred dollars' worth of course-cotton goods, explained Sibley, but with specie, mules, asses, and Spanish blankets in his return inventory, he came back to Missouri as a triumphant entrepreneur and genuine frontier hero.[14]

That being said, the former government factor may have had some personal stake in western Missouri's commercial development and Becknell's journey to Santa Fe. In 1819, two years before Fort Osage factory was closed, Sibley, with the assistance of his father-in-law, began raising hogs and cattle at Fort Osage, constructing a saw and grist mill near there as well. Apparently these were sound economic ventures, for on July 10 of that same year he wrote to his father, Samuel H. Sibley: "An outlet and good market for vast quantities of Flour, Pork and Whiskey will exist for many years among the Traders, Garrisons, &c. on the Missouri and above this [Fort Osage]."[15]

Whether the "&c." referred to Indians is not known; neither is it certain that Sibley actually operated a distillery or engaged in the Indian alcohol trade. But like certain other government officials on the remote Missouri frontier, he understood the monetary potential of the grain and alcohol trade in the vast "wilderness" soon to be visited by William Becknell, and he had no qualms about sharing this information with others.

By early 1824 the movement to clear the land of Indian title immediately west of Fort Osage was gaining momentum. From Fort Osage, no longer a government trading factory, Sibley brought pressure on Senator David Barton of Missouri to support the cession of all Kansa lands in Missouri, that is, all land on the south side of the Missouri River west to the Missouri line, an unquestionable prerequisite to a larger cession to the west. "This fine tract of country is utterly useless to the savages who claim it," he wrote to Senator Barton. The Kansas were willing to sell the tract "for a mere trifle as compared with the immense value of the land," said Sibley, who also spoke of more than a hundred white families squatting on the public domain in central Missouri who had the resources to purchase land but were unwilling to do so for any other land except the tract in question. Allowing "this fine section of country to remain much longer a wilderness," insisted Sibley to Barton, "deserves severe reprehension."[16]

Not to be outdone by Sibley's lobbying of Senator Barton, Senator Benton encouraged and presided over the submission of a memorial (or official proposal by the Missouri general assembly) to the U.S. Senate titled "Proposition to Extinguish Indian Title to Lands in Missouri, drawn up by the General Assembly of the State [of] Missouri." In considerable detail, the memorial complained strongly of such "remnant" tribes as the Shawnees, Peorias, Weas, Delawares, and even Osages (hardly a "remnant" people at 6,000 souls!), whose occupation of certain "small districts" in Missouri was "pregnant with evil to both the Indians themselves and the people of Missouri." Happily, continued the memorial, the Osage and Kansa claims to the enormous tract west of Missouri were only "nominal," and in fact the two tribes actually lived in a few core villages east of the Great Bend of the Arkansas, making their remaining land—what the memorialists also termed "idle" land—useful only for hunting alongside hunters from other tribes.[17]

Why, then, did the Osage and Kansa cession treaties the following year require the two tribes to cede millions of acres of "nominal" or "idle" land (more than 20 million acres in the case of the Kansas alone),[18] extending at some points as far west as present eastern Colorado? Both the Osage Treaty of June 2, 1825, and the Kansa Treaty the following day defined the western boundaries of the two nations at the sources of the Kansas River and its Republican and Smoky Hill tributaries, in present Cheyenne County, Colorado.[19]

One answer: In addition to the intractable determination of white Missourians to clear Missouri of *all* Indians, the government's need to find new reservations for the eastern removal tribes was a driving force behind Senator Benton's memorial to the Senate in 1824. By then it had been decided by Indian Superintendent William Clark in St. Louis and the Office of Indian Affairs in Washington that the eastern tribes would demand to be placed in the more humid area directly west of Missouri (and Arkansas Territory), certainly no farther west than the 98th Meridian near the Great Bend of the Arkansas. But after the land-cession treaties had been signed in early June 1825, what was the need for additional "right-of-way" treaties with the same two nations less than three months later? Even Sibley, who was selected in 1824 by the Office of Indian Affairs to serve on an official survey team for the Santa Fe road and to head a new federal commission for negotiating additional treaties with the Osages and Kansas, questioned the need for such negotiations.[20] Another possible explanation, at least as it related to the Kansas, is that the Kansa leaders who signed the August right-of-way treaty at Sora Kansas Creek (near the Santa Fe road in present central Kansas) were not the same leaders who signed the land-cession treaty in early June; the first signers may have been unaware of the massive Kansa land cession worked out by Superintendent Clark with a different delegation of tribal leaders nearly three months earlier. In his transmittal of the June treaty to the War Department in Washington, Clark stated that every Kansa village was well represented at the St. Louis deliberation. But this could not have been the case. In fact there was only one Kansa village in 1825, and the division into three villages did not take place until 1829 at the earliest.[21]

In any case, the Osage and Kansa right-of-way treaties of August 10 and 16, 1825—at Council Grove and Sora Kansas Creek, respectively—were concluded by Sibley and his fellow commissioners with remarkable dispatch. In addition to granting permission for the United States to survey the actual right-of-way, the Osages and Kansas "on all fit occasions" were bound by the treaties to provide "friendly aid and assistance" to any citizens of the United States and the Republic of Mexico, on or near the overland road, regardless of the circumstances. As well, citizens of the United States and the Mexico republic were to enjoy free access to the overland road "without any hindrance or molestation" on the part of said tribes. But of greater importance for the thousands of Plains Indians who after 1825 continued to hunt on now ceded Osage and Kansa land west of the Great Bend of the Arkansas was Article 4 of the Sibley right-of-way treaties, which further divulged the Indian Affairs Office's support for the Missouri merchants and their well-being along the overland road itself. Article 4 stated: "The Chiefs and Head Men, as aforesaid, do further consent that the road aforesaid shall be considered as extending to a reasonable distance on either side, so that travelers there, at any time, may leave the marked tract, for the purpose of finding subsistence and proper camping places."[22] In other words, the roads to Taos and Santa Fe after mid-August 1825 were more than just the physical spaces needed for horse, mule, and wagon travel; they covered a much larger strip of former Osage and Kansa land upon which any citizen of the United States and Mexico could hunt and camp at their own pleasure—and expect aid and assistance if things went badly.

Rumors (or, occasionally, a more objective account) of Indian depredations on the overland road regularly appeared in Missouri newspapers in 1824, prompting the St. Louis *Enquirer*, then edited by Senator Benton, to complain, "We are tired of repeating this sickening tale."[23] Such reporting was a tactic of Senator Benton and his retinue for securing federal funding of military protection for the Santa Fe traders. In fact, the overland road was relatively peaceful until 1828, when some eighty operators headed for Santa Fe were attacked, resulting in two of their caravans losing several men and $40,000 worth of merchandise,[24] and the authorization the following year of the first U.S. military escort, commanded by Major Bennet Riley.[25] Well in advance of Riley's 1829 infantry escort, which was reasonably successful despite its not being a mounted force,[26] the matter of economy entered into the equation of federal military protection for the traders, as well as for enforcement of the 1802 Act regarding hunting on the recently ceded Kansa and Osage lands. As early as 1819, General Atkinson (then commander of the Ninth Military Department with authority over the entire region west of Missouri) ordered that citizens of the

United States without federal trade licenses were prohibited from hunting anywhere in Indian Country. As a means of enforcing federal law and protecting the Santa Fe traders, Atkinson was open to the idea of a military post at the Great Bend of the Arkansas, midway between western Missouri and Santa Fe, if such could be manned by at least eighty and perhaps as many as a hundred mounted men, ready at all times to pursue depredating parties—Indian or otherwise. But given the insufficient number of troops deployed over the vast western frontier at that time, the cost was prohibitive. Besides, noted General Atkinson, "the traders should be willing and [were] able to protect themselves," especially given the increasing number and size of the caravans headed for New Mexico.[27]

Under such circumstances, what was an unlicensed merchant to do on the road from Missouri to Taos or Santa Fe? They carried trade goods of more than casual interest to thousands of Shawnees, Delawares, Osages, and Kansas west of Missouri, as well as greater numbers of Cheyennes, Arapahoes, Pawnees, Kiowas, Comanches, and Apaches hundreds of miles to the west. An added complication came on May 25, 1824, when Congress required that all traders—even those with licenses—could conduct their business only "at the places thus designated [in their applications for licenses] and at no other places."[28]

For centuries, and in some instances even longer, the lower Missouri Valley Indians had lived in permanent or semipermanent farming villages (unless forced to move by white invaders) that could be designated as "places" for trade. But the Plains Indians were mainly hunters and garden horticulturists with few, if any, "designated" residences that would meet the letter of the 1824 law. Moreover, Indians had second thoughts regarding a road across their lands. Article 19 of the 1802 Act provided that "if the Indians object[ed], the President of the United States [was] authorized to issue a proclamation, prohibiting all traveling of said trace [or road] on Indian land surrounded by settlements of the United States."[29] In the future, would this include the downsized Kansa reservation near Council Grove in 1846?[30] Would it include the numerous other concentrated reserves established in present eastern Kansas after 1825?[31]

On July 14, 1825, more than a month after the Osages signed their land cession treaty in St. Louis and less than a month prior to their right-of-way treaty at Council Grove, a large party of Osages accosted a "good-sized expedition" from Santa Fe at the confluence of the Little and Big Arkansas Rivers, some 50 miles due south of the Santa Fe road, and stole "a great number of Mules, Asses, &c." headed for the Missouri markets. The expedition, with nearly 500 animals, was captained by Bailey Hardeman and comprised American and Mexican traders who also reported the loss of "some other property" and being "illy treated."[32] Under the terms of the forthcoming right-of-way treaty, would these traders have been entitled to receive "aid and assistance" from the very tribes responsible for the thefts and ill treatment?

More assuring for the traders: Only four years after William Becknell left Arrow Rock for New Mexico, the Osages and Kansas had relinquished ownership of much of the actual ground he had covered as well as millions of acres of additional land west of Missouri—a notable accomplishment for George Sibley, William Clark, and the Indian Affairs Office in St. Louis. But a sticky issue remained: No Indians—not even those far distant from the ceded land—had relinquished camping and hunting rights in the trans-Missouri West. Could they have left their hunting and butchering camps temporarily while dealing with the traders on the actual road itself, in a right-of-way "place" guaranteed by treaty and therefore not subject to federal trade and intercourse regulations? By late 1825 a federal survey of the road, mainly the handiwork of Senator Benton, was well under way.

Would this manner of government intervention in the far western Indian Country, heretofore the private realm of venturesome merchants such as Becknell, complement the recent Osage and Kansa treaties and provide the right tools for enforcing federal law in the trans-Missouri West?

4

Benton's Road

Contemporary and less recent histories of the frontier trade between western Missouri and northern New Mexico prior to 1880 (the year the AT&SF railroad was laid to Galisteo Junction a few miles south of Santa Fe) follow a general timeline: 1821–1846, when individual operators and company traders on the Central and Southern Plains turned to alcohol as the principal item of exchange for bison robes harvested by Indians; 1846–1861, including the Mexican-American War and the prebellum years; 1861–1867, the Civil War in the West, relations with native populations, and their postwar consequences; and the years to 1880, often focusing on the AT&SF railroad project.

The focus of this book is 1821–1846 and the related alcohol trade, but later events inform the analysis of this period. A case in point: on February 7, 1849, when Senator Thomas Hart Benton of Missouri rose in the U.S. Senate to declare that, based on ideas he had developed "thirty years before . . . when California was not our own," the time had come to advance trade with Asia by construct-

Thomas Hart Benton, Missouri Senator, 1821–1851. Author (painter) Ferdinand Thomas Lee Boyle, 1861. Wikimedia Commons.

ing a transcontinental railroad funded by the public; bringing private investors into such a grandiose project would only turn it into "a great stock-jobbing business." Understandably, Benton preferred a route directly west of St. Louis along the 38th Parallel, which for the most part followed Becknell's 1821 passage to Santa Fe, but which was discouraged by his son-in-law, John Charles Frémont, on grounds that the 38th Parallel necessitated a difficult if not impossible pass over the rugged Continental Divide west of future Denver. It would also require a connecting link to the 35th Parallel route planned for construction west of Fort Smith—a competing transcontinental line being promoted no less aggressively. Not to worry, Benton assured his fellow Missourians, who were united in their opposition to the link with the 35th to the south. In fact, Benton, whose power in the Senate on economic affairs west of the Mississippi was exceeded by no one in 1849, was focused on one major objective: a transcontinental railroad connecting the middle Mississippi Basin with a port on the Pacific Coast, with a firm understanding that the termini for America's future commerce with the Orient be reserved for the "geographic sisters" of St. Louis and San Francisco. "The rest," he declared, "was a matter of detail."[1]

Well in advance of the Pacific Railroad Surveys of 1853–1855, and more than a decade prior to passage of the Pacific Railroad Act of 1862 that led to the actual construction of transcontinental railroads, Benton was beating his drum for a public-funded line to California following Becknell's first route to Santa Fe, across a land populated by a people he viewed as "untamed and predatory savages, Arabs of the New World, who roamed over the intermediate country of a thousand miles, and considered the merchant and his goods their lawful prey." Benton reported silver, furs, horses, and mules as the items brought to Missouri from New Mexico, but what kinds of merchandise the Missouri traders were taking to New Mexico or points in between he did not mention.[2] In fact, most of the commodities then taken to Santa Fe and the upper Rio Grande Basin, according to the Mexican trader and business magnate Francis X. Aubry, were "flour, ammunition, whiskey, and hardware." Cotton goods were also in demand, said Aubry, and so was "other liquor of all kinds."[3]

Some of the Missouri alcohol consigned for New Mexico never made it to Santa Fe (where Aubry ran a thriving retail alcohol business).[4] Neither was it available in ample supply in the Mexican markets to the south, for the obvious reason that an increasing amount of the controversial commodity was being traded in Indian

Country, at some points between Fort Osage on the western Missouri border and the upper New Mexico settlements at Taos and Santa Fe. Benton's focus, however, remained on railroads and the Asia trade. Yet Indian Agent Benjamin O'Fallon complained to William Clark as early as 1819 of a "brisk whiskey trade" with Indians north and west of Missouri;[5] another in 1824 requested that the Kansa tribe be banned from Missouri—not for any threat they posed to white settlers but for the tribe's own protection from white men who were illegally occupying the tribe's land near the overland road crossing on their own reservation. Neither report elicited a response from the Missouri senator.[6] To the contrary, in an elaboration of the main theme of his earlier speech to his fellow solons, Benton held forth mightily on how the High Plains "Arabs," once the transcontinental railroad was completed, would cast aside feral ways in favor of the comforts of white civilization:

> To the Indians themselves, the opening of a road through their country is an object of vital importance. It is connected with the preservation and improvement of their race. For two hundred years the problem of Indian civilization has been successively presented to each generation of the Americans. . . . Schools have been set up, colleges have been founded, and missions established . . . and after some time, the schools, the colleges, the missions, and the Indians have disappeared together. In the south alone have we seen an exception. . . . It dates its commencement from the opening of *roads* [emphasis added] through their country. Roads induced separate families to settle at the crossing of rivers, to establish themselves at the best springs and tracts of land, and to begin to sell grain and provisions to the travelers, whom, a few years

> before, they would kill and plunder. This imparted the idea of exclusive property in the soil, and created an attachment for a fixed residence. . . . The acquisition of those comforts, relieving the body from the torturing wants of cold and hunger, placed the mind in a condition to pursue its improvement.—This, Mr. President [of the Senate], is the true secret of the happy advance which the southern tribes have made . . . and doubtless, the same cause will produce the same effect among the tribes beyond, which it has produced among the tribes on this side of the Mississippi.[7]

Benton then recounted precedents to back up his case for a "marked" (or surveyed) road and right-of-way west of Missouri through Kansa and Osage domains, then southwest to the upper Rio Grande Basin in New Mexico. These included: (1) a road from Nashville, through the Chickasaw and Choctaw nations, to Natchez, in 1806; (2) three roads through the Cherokee nation, to open trade and intercourse with Georgia, Tennessee, and residents of the lower Mississippi valley, plus twenty more roads to other parts of the United States; (3) and a road from Athens, Georgia, through the Creek lands in 1806, and continued by a congressional act of 1807 "with the consent of the Spanish government, through the then Spanish territory of West Florida to New Orleans."[8]

Strong concerns were voiced in the Senate regarding the marking of the road once it crossed the upper Arkansas and entered Mexico. Nathaniel Macon of North Carolina objected to the road on grounds that, unlike roads east of the Mississippi, which extended through a country of "comparatively civilized Indians," such clearly was not the case west of Missouri, inhabited as it was by Indians who in Macon's view "thought of nothing but killing and robbing a white man the moment they [saw] him." These objections were challenged by Augustus Storrs, Benton's star advocate and prominent Missouri businessman with experience in the New Mexico trade; and by the arrival, in early January 1825, of a memorial from the Missouri General Assembly reporting that American traders were able to compete on equal ground with the Mexican traders in Santa Fe and in other markets to the south.

And indeed such was the case, certainly as it involved alcohol moving across the roads to Taos and Santa Fe. In 1824, for example, northern New Mexico alcohol dealer Marquez y Melo complained bitterly of losing ground to the aggressive American traders. "We all have been unable to sell our wine stocks," he reported, "and not a few of us are sitting tight on full containers and those who tried to empty theirs have lost their principle [*sic*]." Even so, according to the Missouri memorial, the overland trade would be of "incalculable benefit" for the advance of republican institutions throughout Mexico and would contribute to the improvement of the Mexican people in general. Despite strong opposition from some members, the Senate passed Benton's measure by a vote of 30–12; the House responded with a majority in favor. On March 3, 1825, President Monroe signed what many, perhaps most, members of Congress understood to be a *national* bill authorizing a right-of-way from the Indians living there and a well-marked road from western Missouri all the way to the upper Rio Grande Basin in northern New Mexico—an important first link to the Pacific Coast and eventually the Asia markets.[9]

For Benton, certainly, the legislation established a truly national road, one that would become "*the American road* [emphasis added] to India. . . . The European merchant as well as the American," he predicted, "will fly across our continent on a straight line to China

[and] the rich commerce of Asia will flow through our centre." But as Henry Nash Smith has pointed out, the road to the Pacific for Benton was more than just a means of connecting seaports with farmers and merchants in the interior. It was also an instrument of internal development for the trans-Mississippi West, or as Benton put it at the conclusion of his 1849 speech, "An American road to India through the heart of our country will revive upon its line all the wonders of which we have read—and eclipse them. The western wilderness, from the Pacific to the Mississippi, will start into life under its touch." Securing a right-of-way and platting its course by scientific survey under authority of the federal government assured that the road to New Mexico would be truly national, even to the point of the War Department protecting the overland traders from the savages who, hopefully, would one day take up the white man's civilized life.[10]

In fact, the belief that Benton's road was national in scope and purpose has prevailed down to our time. It has been described as an "extension" of the 1811 National (or Cumberland) Road, initially funded by the federal government and subsequently subsidized by some of the states for the purpose of stimulating settlement, agriculture, and commerce to its terminus at the Kaskaskia River in western Illinois.[11] A more recent study characterizes it as "arguably the most successful of the early nineteenth century federal road-building programs which sought to expand commerce and integrate distant regions into the national economy."[12] In 1976 Governor Robert F. Bennett of Kansas advised the U.S. Department of Interior that "the Santa Fe Trail was undoubtedly one of the most significant land routes in the expansion and development of the United States." His appraisal was confirmed by Governor Richard D. Lamm of Colorado that same year,[13] and a subsequent government report on designating the road as a National Historic Trail described it as "one of America's most important commercial routes, established to expedite trade with the Spanish of the Southwest."[14]

Authorizing an official government survey and marking Senator Benton's road transformed Becknell's 1819 route into the first national road in the trans-Missouri West. And beyond that, it was an international road for more than twenty years, even though the Mexican government opposed opening a road from Missouri to Santa Fe "for commercial purposes." Reaffirming his endorsement of Benton's bill, Secretary of State Henry Clay tersely dismissed the Mexican complaint by stating that "an imperfect trace or road, as it is, is now used, and the sole question is, whether it shall be rendered more convenient to the person whose interest or inclination shall induce them to travel it."[15]

Selected by the War Department to head the commission empowered to mark the road was George C. Sibley, who in 1808 had boasted that if war broke out between the United States and England, and Spain entered the fray, "we [the United States] could march there and seize their rich mines in less than 20 days." At the technical level, Dr. John H. Robinson, who had served as cartographer for Zebulon Pike's expedition of 1806 and later as Sibley's deputy Indian agent at Fort Osage, was able to provide important topographical information for Sibley. His fellow commissioners were Thomas Mather and Benjamin Reeves, and with the support of an additional forty men (including head surveyor Joseph C. Brown), fifty-seven horses and mules, seven baggage wagons, and "a good supply of provisions, tools, and ammunition," the expedition left Fort Osage to begin their work on July 17, 1825.[16]

Lacking an abundance of hardwood trees and other natural landmarks for marking, especially as the expedition moved west of

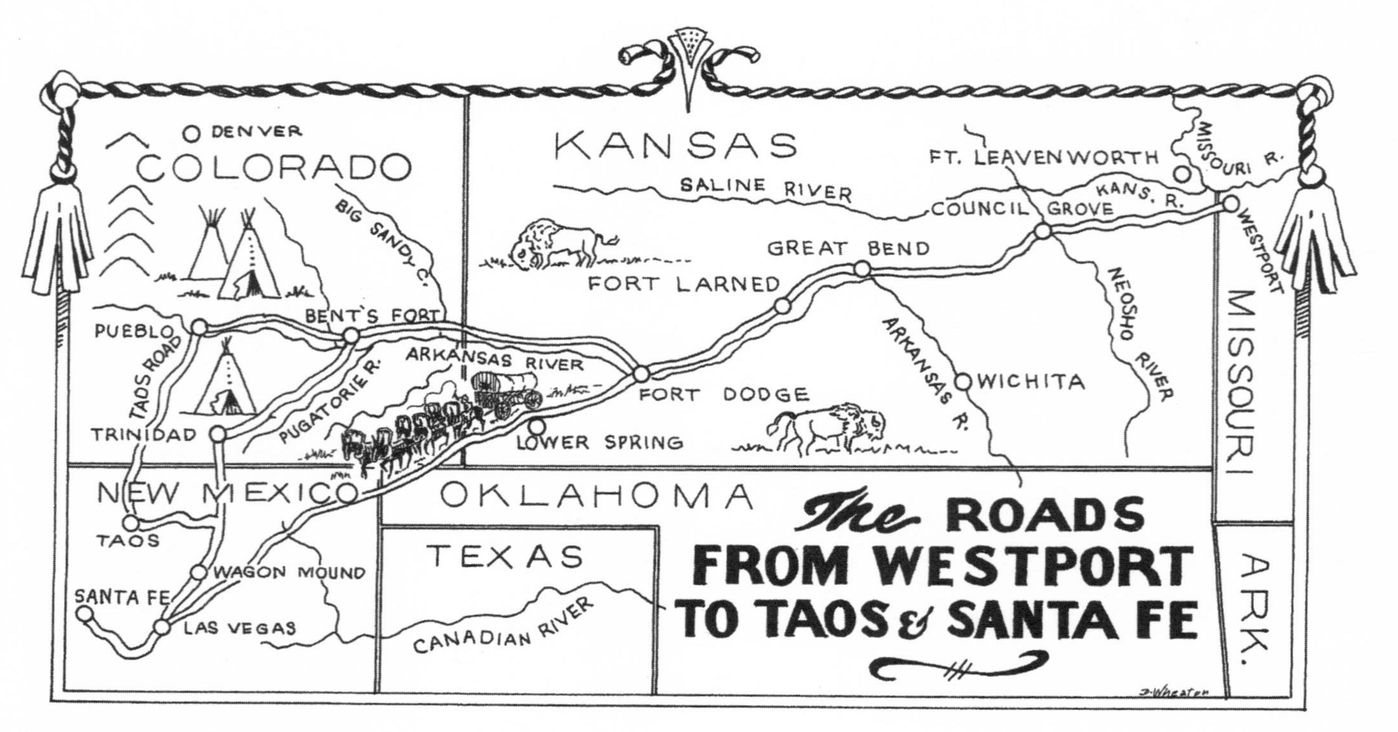

The Roads from Westport to Taos and Santa Fe, 1825

Council Grove and the Neosho Basin, Brown and his assistants marked the road with large posts surrounded by earthen mounds. In the meantime Indian Superintendent Clark in St. Louis informed Mexican authorities in Chihuahua that the United States was marking a road to the international border at the Arkansas River near the 100th Meridian and was considering establishing a military post near there to protect the road.[17] By September 11 the expedition arrived at what they believed was the 100th Meridian and camped, awaiting permission to proceed with the survey into Mexico Territory. None came and so it was decided that a detachment of Sibley, Brown, and William S. "Old Bill" Williams would continue on to Taos, and possibly to Santa Fe as well, to secure the needed authority to extend the survey into New Mexico. In October they reached Taos,[18] but it was not until June 16, 1826, that permission was granted by Mexican authorities to "examine" but not to "mark" the road from Taos northeast to the Arkansas River. This Sibley and Brown completed without incident on September 16 that same year. Less than a year later, from mid-May to late July 1827, Sibley and a smaller party made corrections in the eastern portion of the 1825 survey, including the construction of a large earthen mound around a prominently displayed post on the boundary between Missouri and Indian Country. In addition to the flour, cornmeal, salt, and bacon Sibley loaded on government wagons for the 1827 journey was a keg of whiskey, a commodity soon in high demand on the recently marked roads.[19]

The marking bill of March 3, 1825, mostly fulfilled Senator Benton's wish list for the overland route. Considering the debate it engendered, the Osage and Kansa right-of-way issue easily eclipsed the surveying and marking issue. As it turned out, neither tribe challenged the de facto location of the road—that was left to other tribes farther west. During the debate Senator Richard M. Johnson of Kentucky supported the rights-of-way proposal as an effective means for protecting an "inland branch of trade" that certainly was no less important than "lighthouses or $500,000 to suppress piracy in the West Indies." On one hand, his colleague William Kelly of Alabama agreed by proclaiming that for the overland commerce "to be safe, a road must be had—a right of way—'*a trace,*' if you please."[20] On the other hand, a recent study of High Plains freighting covering the period after 1821 pronounced the marking of the overland trail a "wasted effort,"[21] and a related study focusing on the market revolution west of Missouri after 1808 contended that marking the road was much less Commissioner Sibley's real mission than it was to secure the all-important rights-of-way.[22]

Most of the wagon trains to Taos and Santa Fe after mid-September 1825 ignored Sibley's markers in favor of wheel ruts, river crossings, butchering sites, and other roadside debris left by others. It was not long before the marker posts were damaged or destroyed and the mounds eroded due to weather, buffalo wallowing, curious travelers, and Indians. In fact, Sibley himself admitted that the markers were no improvement over those left by the wagons and "would be soon thrown down."[23] That being said, the survey and marking *did* figure prominently in the August 10 and 16 treaties, and Congress *did* provide Sibley and his fellow commissioners $10,000 for surveying, setting up posts, and piling up sod—all the way from Fort Osage to the international boundary to the west. So why negotiate with the Osages and Kansas for something that was of little consequence to the future of the overland road and trade?

A possible explanation recalls the Osage and Kansa right-of-way treaties dated June 2 and 3, 1825. Article I of the Great and Little Osage Treaty, negotiated on August 10, 1825, by Sibley at Coun-

Copy of "A Citadel of the Plains." Artist Frederic Remington's drawing of Pawnee Rock, a landmark on the Santa Fe road a few miles southwest of the Great Bend of the Arkansas, in Colonel Henry Inman, The Old Santa Fe Trail *(1897). Courtesy of David Dary.*

cil Grove on the upper Neosho, stated: "The Chiefs and Head Men of the Great and Little Osages, for themselves and their nations, respectively, do consent and agree that the Commissioners of the United States shall and may survey and mark out a road, in such manner as they may think proper, through any of the territory owned or claimed by the said Great and Little Osage nations."[24] The companion agreement with the Kansas, at Sora Kansas Creek near present McPherson, Kansas, six days later was a near verbatim copy of the Osage agreement. What is important here is that the cession treaties of June 2 and 3 were not proclaimed law until December 30, 1825, prompting a worried Sibley to record in his journal the day after the Osage parley at Council Grove: "The Chiefs & principal [Osage] all went away perfectly satisfied, as well they might, for the Commissioners allowed them very liberally, as I think, for the Right of Way through the country claimed by them, as *their* right, that is at best a doubtful one, if the Treaty [of June 2] lately signed by them [the Osages] at St. Louis, with General Clark, is ratified and confirmed by Congress."[25]

What concerned Sibley (and surely Benton, who admitted that his bill was "a novel and strange subject," requiring him "to lay a foundation of facts, to furnish a reason and argument for everything that was asked"[26]) was Senate opposition to the land-cession bill (which passed by only two votes);[27] this opposition led to the August 10 and 16 backup treaties, providing the mechanism (as well as funding) for gathering the legal data proving unequivocally the existence of a bona fide national road connecting Missouri and Mexico.

Indeed, it was an extraordinary government road. Unlike most eastern roads, which in the planning or developmental stages called for specific legal location, maximum grades, width of actual roadway, bridges, and hard surfacing prior to receiving federal or state authorization or funding, the roads to Taos and Santa Fe were wholly unimproved and outright primitive by comparison.[28] Because of the open and generally level terrain west of Council Grove and east of the Raton Mountains, the actual roadbeds were placed wherever the wagon masters found it least difficult and dangerous to drive (keeping in mind at all times, of course, the amount of grass and water available and the location of natural markers such as the Neosho River crossing at Council Grove, the Great Bend of the Arkansas, Pawnee Rock, Chouteau's Island, Point of Rocks, Wagon Mound, and so on). In fact, Sibley's mounds and posts had more to do with Indian relations and Indian policy in the trans-Missouri West than with the government providing a dependable guideway to Taos and Santa Fe.

5

Regulation Revisited

In early 1866, Senator James Grimes of Iowa attached an amendment to the annual Indian appropriation bill providing that "any moral and loyal citizen" who posted a $5,000 to $10,000 bond could secure, from a federal district judge or U.S. attorney, a license for engaging in Indian trade.[1] The amendment became law on July 26, 1866, with little fanfare in the Senate and even less among the public at large. For Americans, wearied by civil war, obtaining a more permissive law for Indian traders was not a high priority. By 1866 most Indians were on the threshold of being forced onto concentrated reservations, where most commercial transactions would take place at federally sanctioned and government-run stores. That setting was not much different from the government trade factories prior to 1822.

This is not to say that Indian trade was devoid of any regulation during the interim. The requirement of a federal license to trade with Indians dated to the Indian Trade and Intercourse Act of July 22, 1790, and had been supplemented by the subsequent Trade Acts of 1793, 1796, and 1802, all of which remained in force well beyond the demise of the factory system. Indeed, private traders operating in the remote West beyond the Mississippi River after 1822 were granted licenses for up to seven years, five more that the standard two years allowed for others.[2] In addition, Section 4 of a law passed on May 25, 1824, required: "That it be the duty of Indian agents to designate, from time to time, certain *convenient* [emphasis added] and suitable places for carrying on trade with the different Indian tribes, and to require all traders to trade at the places thus designated, and *at no other places* [emphasis added]."[3]

Section 2 of that same law authorized the President to appoint "suitable persons for commissioners" (i.e., for surveying and marking an overland road to New Mexico), and to provide $10,000 for negotiating with Indians "beyond the Mississippi." Section 6 authorized an additional $10,000 for military protection for the Osage and Kansa commissioners, but only "if needed." A little more than a year later, on July 6, 1825, with the Cheyenne nation congregated at the mouth of the Teton (Bad) River in present South Dakota, Brigadier General Henry Atkinson and Indian Agent Benjamin O'Fallon negotiated the first peace and friendship treaty with the Cheyennes. Not unexpectedly, but remarkable nonetheless for its compatibility with Section 4 of the 1824 licensing law, was Section 3 of the Teton River treaty, which read: "All trade and intercourse with the Cheyenne tribe shall be transacted at such place or places as may be *designated* [emphasis added] and pointed out by the President of the United States, through his agents; and none but American citizens duly authorized by the United States, shall be admitted to trade or hold intercourse with said tribe."[4]

But designated for whom? For the Cheyenne people soon to call the upper Arkansas Basin their home? For the Osages and

Kansas on their much reduced lands west of Missouri? For private traders no longer under the watchful eyes of government factors? For the Missouri Shawnees, forced to take up a new life on a reservation traversed by a government road leading to New Mexico? For Senator Benton and his crowd? For venturesome traders persuaded that, given the increasing demand for bison robes in the 1820s, the High Plains economy might one day be integrated into the national marketplace?

How one answered was contingent on the quality of law enforcement in Indian Country, defined in the Indian Trade and Intercourse law of 1802 as all land west of an irregular line running south of the mouth of the Cuyahoga River at Lake Erie to the middle point of St. Mary's River, on the Georgia-Florida border, with the important qualifier that "if the boundary line between said Indian tribes and the United States shall, at any time hereafter, be varied, by any treaty which shall be made between the said Indian tribes and the United States, then all provisions in this act shall be construed to apply to said line so to be varied, in the same manner as said provisions apply, by force of this act, to the boundary herein before recited."[5]

The detailed yet roundabout wording of the 1802 law emboldened most traders and their suppliers to obtain licenses from the St. Louis superintendency for convenient trade centers west of Missouri. In 1825, Superintendent Clark issued licenses to Joshua Pilcher, Lucien Fontenelle, William Vanderburgh, Andrew Dripps, and Charles Bent (as successors to the assets of the old Missouri Fur Company); to Bernard Pratte, Auguste P. Chouteau, and Bartholomew Berthold Company; and to Russel Farnham and Michel Robidoux—all to "trade with Indians" near the mouth of the Kansas River, a short distance from Westport Landing on the

William Clark, St. Louis Indian Superintendent, 1822–1839. Author (painter) Charles Willson Peale, 1810. Wikimedia Commons.

Missouri River and the nearby town of Westport, which in the late 1820s was displacing Independence as the favored point of outfitting for the overland trip to New Mexico.[6] In early April 1831 John Gantt and partner Jefferson Blackwell were issued a license to trade with the Cheyennes and Arapahoes on the Platte River,[7] and on December 13, 1834, Charles Bent with his brother William and Ceran St. Vrain representing the recently organized firm of Bent, St. Vrain & Co. were authorized to trade at three separate locations, with six different tribes. Their license read:

> To Charles Bent for two years, with twenty-nine men employed, at Fort William [later renamed Bent's Fort, near present La Junta, CO] on the north side of the Arkansas, about 40 miles east of the Rocky mountains, about twenty miles north of the Spanish Peaks, and about five miles below one of the principal forks of the Arkansas; at Union point, on the north side of the Arkansas, near the foot of the Rocky Mountains, about ten miles below the Black Hills, and at a point near the mouth of Bear river, on the waters of the Grand river of the Colorado River of the West, with the Arapahoes, Cheyennes, Kiowas, Snakes, Sioux, and Arickaras.[8]

The contrast between the Gantt-Blackwell and Bent licenses should not go unnoticed. Gantt and Blackwell were authorized to trade with two tribes at one very general location; Bent and his associates were authorized to trade with six tribes at three locations, each described in considerable detail. Less than a month after receiving their license, Gantt and Blackwell (and seventy of their employees) brazenly breached it by trading with certain unidentified Indians—clearly not Cheyennes or Arapahoes—at the mouth of the Kansas River for "three or four days."[9] The fact that no judicial action was initiated against their bonds by federal authorities in nearby Missouri surely did not go unnoticed by the individuals and firms operating at remote points near the mouth of Bear River and along the wagon roads to Taos and Santa Fe.

Under the Indian Trade and Intercourse Act of 1802, the president of United States was authorized to "prevent or restrain the vending or distribution of spirituous liquors among all or any of said Indian tribes";[10] and in an amendment to the 1822 Act it was further provided that territorial governors serving as Indian superintendents, as well as War Department and Indian Office officials, were authorized to search for and seize "ardent spirits" in the possession, or rumored to be in the possession, of traders operating in Indian Country. Confiscated goods were to be divided equally between those who had seized them (or served as informants) and the federal government, and the bonds of licensed traders guilty of the infraction could be placed in suit.[11] Whether the Gantt-Blackwell trade goods in 1831 at the mouth of the Kansas and the Taos and Santa Fe roads included "ardent spirits" is not known. A report that John Gantt was trading alcohol with the Cheyennes in the Platte River basin not long thereafter, however, makes it difficult to believe that alcohol was not a commodity. In any case, the government's obvious laxity in oversight near a major river, easily connecting the area with St. Louis and a federal judicial center there, was not lost on traders dealing with Indians in the upper Arkansas Basin hundreds of miles to the southwest.

By 1829 the Missouri Shawnees had taken up residence on the government reservation granted them in 1825, directly west of Missouri, where the Santa Fe road crossed the state line and passed west across more than 30 miles of the tribal land. Certainly the Shawnees were not unfamiliar with alcohol when they first arrived near the mouth of the Kansas. One traveler who visited them in southeastern Missouri in the early 1800s reported that the once "virtuous" Shawnees, responding to the habits of the hard-drinking white neighbors who surrounded them, were given to excessive drinking, causing not a few to become "degenerated."[12] Whether they might still be indulging in such habits on the new reservation—perhaps at an even more alarming rate—was the subject of correspondence between the Fort Leavenworth Indian Agency and Indian Office officials in Washington. The correspondence provides a record for better understanding the deadly dealing of alcohol traders on the roads to Taos and Santa Fe.

Writing to Indian Commissioner Elbert Herring in the spring of 1833, Fort Leavenworth Agent Richard Cummins acknowledged having recently received instructions to "seize the article [alcohol] whenever and wherever found within this agency & deposit the same at the nearest military post, & etc." This, responded Cummins, was a difficult instruction to carry out. Extending south along the state line for a distance of 60–70 miles were numerous distillers and dealers eager to accommodate the Shawnees and their drinking habits, continued Cummins. But for a dependable supply of alcohol the Shawnees preferred the overland traders near the mouth of the Kansas, for the simple reason that they were "more easy" to deal with. Moreover, in the area around Westport and the mouth of the Kansas, it was difficult if not impossible to find whites living there willing to testify in a grand jury proceeding against non-Indians accused of engaging in the illicit alcohol trade. "I can assure you," emphasized Cummins, "that one or two men [he and his sub-agent] have a sorry chance to manage these rusty fellows. I mean the whites, for they generally 'go Indian' with a butcher knife & etc. and my sub-agent is an old man, very ineffective and not able to render much assistance."[13]

By the late 1820s and early 1830s the Shawnees were not alone as customers for overland traders who eagerly developed a local market while outfitting for the long journey to Taos and Santa Fe. In fact, this market for alcohol grew by leaps and bounds during the next decade. As part of the government's Indian removal program, a band of Ohios and Missouri Delawares were relocated to a point near the Shawnee reservation in 1829. In 1832 the Missouri Kickapoos agreed to a reservation just north of the Shawnees and

Delawares, and that same year the Kaskaskias, Weas, Peorias, and Piankashaws from Illinois were placed in areas directly south of Shawnee and Delaware lands.[14] Thus from 1829 through 1832 several thousand additional Indians were settled adjacent to or within a few miles of the overland road to New Mexico, a number that by 1846 had increased to some 10,000 new arrivals onto the eastern flank of Indian Country. Of paramount interest to the traders: All of these newly arrived Indians held annuity contracts resulting from their removal agreements with the government that, according to one account of the burgeoning Kansas City economy, allowed them $1 million collectively of discretionary spending per year.[15]

Added to the emigrant tribes were the Kansas, then residing on their diminished reservation west of Topeka, due north of the overland road. Here they regularly consumed "large quantities of whiskey from Missouri," wrote Kansa Agent Marston G. Clark to his superiors, and it was time for the government to take the Indian trade "back into its own hands and away from the traders whose extortion and seduction has so demoralized these Indians."[16] But this was out of the question given the recent failure of the factory system and the powerful opposition of Senator Benton and well-funded trade firms, such as the American Fur Company, operating in the upper Missouri country, and Bent, St. Vrain & Co., trading with the Indians along the Platte and the upper Arkansas. Thus, the emerging consensus in Washington was to make Indian trade regulations more restrictive and to define more precisely just *how* and *where* new regulations were to be enforced if at all possible.

A thorny problem, however, were the drinking habits of boatmen employed by the American Fur Company for operations among Indians of the upper Missouri. Accustomed to drinking as part of a daily routine, most of the boatmen—like their Irish canaller counterparts who were issued three to four jiggers of whiskey a day during working hours[17]—were reluctant to work without imbibing on the job. Thus to circumvent the law against taking alcohol into Indian Country it finally came down to Indian superintendents, with the permission of the president of the United States, issuing special permits for the fur companies "to take into the Indian Country, whiskey for the use of the Boatmen employed by them to assist in Trade; limiting the quantity to the number of hands employed, and the time they are to be absent, and taking bond that it is not to be sold, bartered, or given to Indians." But in practice it was otherwise. Indian Superintendent William Clark wrote to his superiors in Washington in the fall of 1831:

> Under this authority, and comfortable thereto that permits have been granted to the Traders—and relying on their good faith, it was not deemed necessary to examine their outfits, nor were their bonds inspected by the officers of the day or the military posts on their routes—this delicate task was dispensed with. Within a few days past, however, I have received information on this subject to convince me that the privilege of the Boatmen has been abused. . . . Alcohol has been taken [into Indian Country] which it seems, after being reduced, has been furnished to the Indians by the gallon keg![18]

Not surprisingly, the question was raised by the Taos and Santa Fe traders as to whether similar special permits should not also be issued to teamsters and wagon hands laboring on the overland roads to Mexico. These roads, after all, had been surveyed and marked by the national government and, in the view of most Indian traders in St. Louis and at the mouth of Kansas to the west, were truly national in scope—certainly as much as the mighty Missouri River to the northwest. Apart from the technical skills involved, what were the differences between oarsmen pushing boats up a river through Indian Country, versus teamsters driving mules and wagons over a national road, also through Indian Country? Why were the former allowed alcohol for their labor but the latter were not?

In the absence of any discussion in Congress over such questions, a consensus developed for simply moving beyond restricting alcohol to removing the supposed nefarious commodity absolutely from the Indians' grasp, thereby discouraging or, hopefully, eradicating their "passion for passing through life in a state of perpetual delirium," as one English scientist sized up the matter.[19] Following a short but spirited debate that focused on the excessive workload of the Indian Office, which by 1830 had issued nearly a hundred trade licenses (and accompanied by reports of so many violations that the traders as a group were no longer viewed as trustworthy), the outcome was the passage, on July 9, 1832, of a law providing that "no ardent spirits shall be hereafter introduced, under any pretense, into the Indian country."[20]

Two years later the Indian Trade and Intercourse Act of 1834 addressed the problem that had plagued the Indian Office in Washington and government officials on the western frontier since 1802: the array of land-cession treaties that too often left federal officials in doubt as to where, at a particular time, the legal boundaries of Indian Country actually were. After June 30, 1834, there was little room for doubt, certainly not where a national road connected Missouri and northern New Mexico. Section 1 of the 1834 Act stated: "That all that part of the United States west of the Mississippi, and not within the states of Missouri and Louisiana, or the Territory of Arkansas, and also, that part of the United States

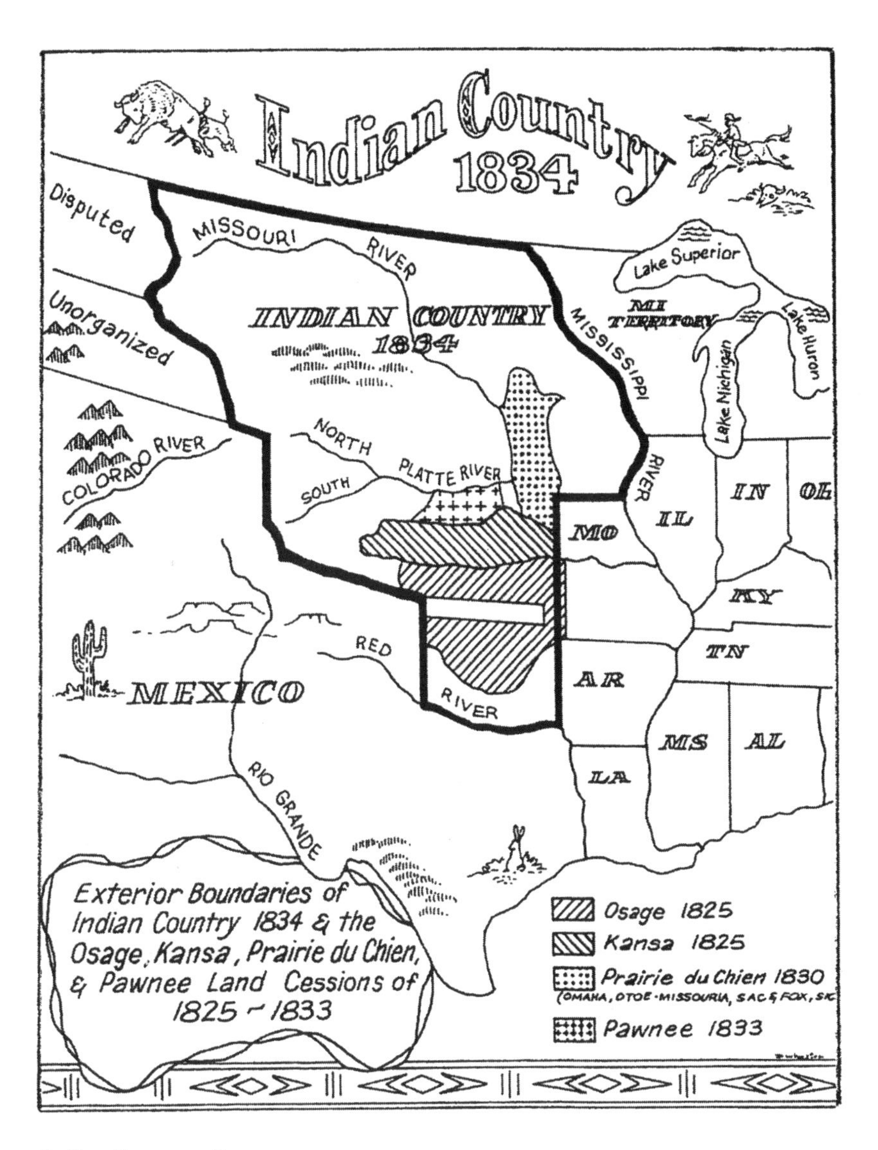

Indian Country, 1834

east of the Mississippi River, and not within the state to which the Indian title has not been extinguished, for the purpose of this act, be taken and deemed to be Indian country."[21]

Surprisingly, the new law increased the penalty for selling alcohol to Indians only slightly, to a fine of $500 for those who traded alcohol with the Indians, and $300 for those who were actually apprehended for trying to engage in such a transaction. In fact, very few of the traders who were aware of the large profits to be derived from trading alcohol for bison robes were deterred by the 1834 law.

The Shawnees living alongside the road to Taos and Santa Fe were not deterred either. In a speech at a "private" meeting with Western Indian Superintendent Francis W. Armstrong, an unnamed Shawnee chief admitted that most of his people knew that whiskey was "bad" for them. But some of his younger men had been told by white traders at Independence that "there was no law against Indians taking whiskey into their country, and [that] nobody said so except their Agent [Richard Cummins] and bad men at the Fort [Leavenworth]." In other words, the Shawnee leader's position was that Indians under the 1834 and all previous Indian alcohol restrictions might legally engage in the alcohol trade with their own people and other Indians as well. In fact, some of the younger Shawnees had been told they could take whiskey to their agent's house and not be punished, and if they were arrested and jailed, other white men "would go and let them out again." Said the Shawnee chief, "We are sorry, my Father, that this is so—but we have no laws [regarding alcohol] and our great Father does not put into execution the laws he makes."[22] It was an important turn of events. But by then most of the traders were wondering if the road to New Mexico was, or ever had been, an actual a part of Indian Country.

6

Benton Vindicated

Congressional passage of a general Indian removal bill in 1830,[1] followed by a supplementary law in 1834[2] providing that all of the United States west of the Mississippi River not in the states of Missouri and Louisiana or Arkansas Territory be designated as "Indian country," prompted hope among government officials that Indians in this region (and possibly some eastern removal Indians as well) might one day be assimilated into the mainstream of American life. In this regard, Senator Thomas Hart Benton's efforts to reconfigure an overland trail first used by Indians and then by non-Indian traders into a national road between Missouri and Mexico provided encouragement and possible justification for additional changes in federal Indian policy.

If, for example, the flow of commerce between the United States and Mexico was supplemented by markets along the way, would this not promote the prosperity and permanence of Indian Country? Responding to reports of Indian attacks along the road in late 1827, and more so in the summer and fall of 1828,[3] overland traders received a boost in morale when the War Department, under the order of President Andrew Jackson himself, dispatched four companies of the 6th Regiment, United States Infantry, to escort the spring caravan headed for New Mexico. Commanded by Major (Brevet) Bennet Riley, the four companies were somewhat hampered in their operations because, unlike Indians, they were unmounted. Even so, the caravan of 1829 experienced no major Indian difficulties while under the protection of Major Riley's infantry. Not surprisingly, then, Senator Benton in Washington made the most of it, submitting Major Riley's official report to the Senate in 1830, primarily as a means of garnering legislative support for greater military protection—this time mounted, of course—for the overland road.[4] Could not the deployment of greater military force counter Indians who harassed the traders and stole from the wagons? Could it not turn the "savages" away from the life of the chase in favor of a settled agrarian existence, that is, the raising of grain and other foodstuffs for sale to the overland traders and travelers and even to other Indians? Could this provide proof that individual family farms and a "settled existence" were the keys to a "cheering progress in the arts of civilization," as Benton had so passionately suggested in 1825?[5]

Considering the status of early–nineteenth-century agricultural technology in relation to the average annual precipitation west of present Kansas City, it might have been possible for the removal Indians and perhaps even some of the nearby Pawnees, Kansas, and Osages to engage in limited agricultural production. Near the mouth of the Kansas River, where the Missouri Shawnees were placed by the government in 1825, the average annual rainfall was nearly forty inches. West of the 100th Meridian and on into present eastern Colorado, however, the average annual rainfall was less than sixteen inches (and in some years half that amount). It could be folly for a U.S. senator from a far western state most closely associated with the overland commerce advising his fellow solons that any Indian family in 1830 could survive on a High Plains farm, let alone produce surplus commodities for sale to others.[6]

Nevertheless, Benton's efforts to promote a national road from Missouri to New Mexico on grounds that it would cause the Indians to refrain from plundering and killing in favor of a sedentary existence and selling the fruits of their own labor to others[7] did call attention, perhaps inadvertently, to the possibility that an internal trade (i.e., goods produced and traded in Indian Country) might be a more effective means of promoting the new road. There were the large western Comanche trade fairs at Big Timbers on the mountain route to Taos and Santa Fe, some 20 miles below the mouth of the Purgatoire, that regularly attracted thousands of Indian traders. Through exchange links, these connected to near and distant Mexican markets, as well as the Mandan and Hidatsa trade citadels in the Missouri Valley and the more remote mustang pastures of the central and southern Rocky Mountains.[8] Indeed, a thriving internal trade network might lead to the establishment and growth of new commercial centers along overland roads, which in turn would attract more Indians and, perhaps, white settlers as well. But as we see below, attracting venturesome white men and their families to this new land of promise was tempered and in some cases prohibited by certain requirements of the 1832 and 1834 Indian Country laws. These included:

— The requirement of having a federal license for all trade with Indians;

— The requirement to trade with Indians only at designated places in Indian Country;
— A $500 fine for non-Indians hunting or trapping on all Indian lands, based on a treaty with the United States, and the forfeiture of all traps, guns, and ammunition in the violator's possession;
— A $2,000 fine for asserting any contravention or infraction of any Indian Country treaty;
— A $500 fine for selling, exchanging, giving, bartering, or disposing of any spirituous liquor or wine to an Indian in the Indian Country; and
— A $1,000 fine for setting up and operating a distillery in Indian Country for manufacturing ardent spirits.[9]

The last regulation, involving distilleries, was a major concern for the Taos and Santa Fe traders, given the numerous distilleries cropping up near the eastern and western boundaries of Indian Country defined by the 1834 law. Leading the distillers on the eastern flank was James Hyatt McGee, who set up a large grist mill and distillery at Westport in 1827. Earlier, in 1824, Thomas L. "Peg-leg" Smith had traveled from Franklin to Santa Fe with Alexander La Grande's caravan; soon thereafter, in association with James Baird and Samuel Chambers, he established what may have been the first commercial distillery in Taos. Two years later William Workman at Taos wrote his brother David in Missouri that he and Mathew Kincaid had purchased a large quantity of wheat and corn and requested that David ship them two 80-gallon stills for the distillery they were planning to build. And by 1832 Simon Turley's large mill and distillery was in full production at Arroyo Hondo, a few miles north of Taos. This dramatic increase in alcohol production in northern New Mexico was matched by a similar surge on the eastern border of Indian Country. Writing to the commissioner of Indian Affairs in 1833, Fort Leavenworth Indian Agent Richard Cummins reported, "I cannot give you a correct idea of the numbers engaged in the [alcohol] trade, but commencing at the Missouri River, they are settled near the [state] line for a distance of sixty or seventy miles. . . . [T]his class of people & their friends are numerous [and] are all most daily dealing out the article to the Indians."[10]

In the meantime, the amount of American merchandise shipped over the roads to Taos and Santa Fe increased significantly. According to veteran Santa Fe trader and journalist Josiah Gregg, the value of goods transported to New Mexico in 1822 was $15,000; by 1828 it had increased to $150,000; in 1831 it was up to $250,000; and by the early 1840s it had increased to nearly a half-million dollars. In 1828 Gregg reported that a hundred wagons were heading west; by 1843 that number had increased to 230.[11]

Nonalcoholic merchandise transported to the Taos and Santa Fe region included axes, knives, miscellaneous hardware, guns, powder, blankets, silks, and dry goods of varying quality; shipments east to Missouri included bullion, specie, furs, mules, horses, asses, coarse woolens, and animal robes and skins. Because specie was generally in short supply in developing frontier states such as Missouri, reports of gold and silver obtained in Mexico by American traders were always welcome news. In Fayette, Missouri, in the summer of 1837, it was reported that a certain Mr. White's company had secured between $80,000 and $100,000 in gold dust and silver bars in northern New Mexico; in Boone county, Missouri, in summer 1840, the overland trade firm of Hicks and Marney had obtained $200,000 in bullion and specie, with one wagon alone from Chihuahua bringing $50,000 in bullion and $30,000 in specie.[12]

Alcohol became a major and highly profitable commodity in the overland trade between 1825—when the roads to Taos and Santa Fe first became "national"[13]—and the outbreak of the Mexican-American War two decades later. While there is no arguing that the commodity did attract some dealers whose intensions and business tactics were questionable at best, it also was a popular trade item for venturesome entrepreneurs with much less odious intent. Certainly by the time overland trade began melding into the regional and national markets in the early 1830s, alcohol was viewed as a reputable trade item by most individual operators. This was also true of many firms whose operations were reliant on the services of suppliers, brokerage houses, and other financial institutions far removed from where alcohol transactions took place. Whether Senator Benton and his crowd were aware of the immense financial potential of the alcohol trade is unclear, but the dramatic growth of the distillery industries in western Missouri and northern Mexico suggests that opening roads across the prairies and plains as a means of preserving and improving the condition of Indians warrants careful consideration.

Several forces converged in the post-1825 period to embolden traders to consider using alcohol as a major trade item on the roads to Taos and Santa Fe. For one thing, white Americans were then consuming alcohol at record rates. Counting men, women, and children (above age fifteen), the average per capita intake of distilled alcohol in the early 1830s was five gallons per year—seven gallons, if beer, wine, and hard cider were included.[14] Amounting to a consumption level fully three times that of twentieth-century America,[15] it is not surprising that such habits prompted one distiller (who, like many of his fellow Americans, considered corn whiskey far superior to anything Europeans could possibly imagine or hope to produce) to insist that the fluid commodity be dubbed the national beverage of choice.[16]

In short, antebellum America was a drinking nation with unusually high levels of individual consumption, leading one historian of the topic to designate the United States during the early national period as "the Alcoholic Republic." Was there anything inherently wrong in an enterprising trader skirting or even ignoring federal regulations devised by misguided government officials to prohibit alcohol as a trade item, in a remote region where a significant demand for the product existed? If government officials themselves used the commodity as a tool for implementing national Indian policy—which of course they did with little restraint[17]—why shouldn't a private trader have a go at it as well?

Certainly alcohol was a credible profit option, if measured by the economic opportunities presented by Benton's recently designated national road. But there were changes in the air. Not long after wagons began moving in greater numbers over the roads to northern New Mexico, the harvesting of beaver and other small animal pelts declined dramatically in the American Southwest, resulting in a drastic decline in the shipment of such commodities to eastern and international markets. The causes were several: aggressive trapper depletion, leading to natural recovery falling behind in the number of live animals available for harvesting; lessening demand for furs thanks to the vagaries of fashion on a global basis; higher Mexican tariffs on products exchanged for small-animal furs; a dramatic increase in demand for bison robes and other coarse-hair animal skins, resulting from their relatively low cost and functional value for keeping warm and comfortable in low

Southern Cheyenne Indians trading alcohol for buffalo robes with Kiowas in western Kansas following their flight from Colorado Territory in 1861. From Harper's New Monthly Magazine *39 (1869): 25.*

temperature environments; and enormous profits to be had from the bison trade if a dependable and cheap source of labor for killing and preparing the robes for market could be developed.[18] And last, but certainly not least, a safe and convenient route for moving the heavy and increasingly valuable robes to market became available compliments of Senator Benton and his aides. What remained was to recruit native people in large enough numbers to fulfill the plan, which in the end would constitute proof that Benton's strategy for civilizing a savage people was dependent on establishing a national road through their own country.[19]

As we have seen, the Kansa and Osage nations in present eastern and central Kansas granted right-of-way privileges to the actual road site in 1825 and were granted smaller and more concentrated reservations nearby, as were several emigrant tribes from the East soon thereafter. Farther west, on the High Plains of present western Kansas and eastern Colorado, it was a different matter. Not until 1851 did the Cheyenne and Arapaho peoples have a legal claim (established by a treaty with the United States) to the overland road country;[20] in the case of the Comanches, Kiowas, and Plains Apaches, such was not the case until 1853. Article 3 of the Comanche, Kiowa, and Apache Treaty, finalized in late July that year a few miles west of present Dodge City, Kansas, provided that "the aforesaid Indian tribes do also hereby recognize and acknowledge the right of the United States to lay off and mark out road or highways . . . within *territories inhabited* [emphasis added] by the said tribes,"[21] which at the time lay immediately south of the Arkansas River. Prior to the treaty ending the Mexican-American War in 1848, however, their country west of the 100th Meridian was still part of Mexico. And until the celebrated "Great Peace of 1840"[22] (the Cheyennes and Arapahoes on the one side and the Comanches, Kiowas, and Plains Apaches on the other) the two groups were on unfriendly terms and thus averse to mustering a collective workforce in support of a large bison robe business that seemed imminent along the American portion of the Taos and Santa Fe roads. By the late 1820s it was apparent that the Cheyennes and a lesser number of Arapahoes were the ones to answer the trader's call on the upper Arkansas.

To the east, the Kansas increased their raiding on the overland trains and, with annuities provided by the land-cession treaty of 1825, emerged as major suppliers of alcohol to other Indians—alcohol the Kansas either seized from overland traders or obtained for

Street scene in Council Grove in the 1870s. Courtesy of Kansas State Historical Society.

cash from distillers in western Missouri. In 1833, Kansa agent Marston G. Clark reported that large quantities of whiskey from western Missouri were being consumed by the Kansas; simultaneously, they were engaged in an extensive "traffick" with other Indians in present eastern Kansas. One veteran traveler with a caravan headed for Santa Fe carrying twenty-four barrels of alcohol "designated for the Indian trade" reported that "the whole [Kansa] nation is in nowise remiss in their devotion to whiskey," prompting the Indian Office in Washington to inveigh against the Kansas as some of the worst "dealers and drinkers" west of Missouri.[23]

And well they might be, as newly appointed Kansa agent John Montgomery learned in 1855. Apparently unfamiliar with the politics of trade and alcohol along the road to New Mexico, Montgomery reported,

> As I have been with the Kansas Indians but a short time it is impossible for me to make a full and lengthy report on their condition, progress, etc. They do have an annuity of ten thousand dollars which after being paid to them is mostly laid out for provisions and whiskey, and for the latter a considerable amount of this annuity is spent, and of which there is a full supply here and in the Territory, they drink it where and whenever they can get it.[24]

What concerned Agent Montgomery most was that the Kansas were trying to survive on a 20-by-20-mile reservation at Council Grove, situated "on one of the greatest thoroughfares of the west."[25] Given the tribe's record of begging for, stealing, and trading in alcohol, why had the Kansas been forced to move once again in 1846? This time it was to an even smaller reservation abutting and, according to some accounts, surrounding the entire Council Grove town site, which by then was the most important government outfitting, repair, and supply facility on the overland road between western Missouri and the international boundary hundreds of miles to the west. Was the action simply an unfortunate response to Senator Benton's plan for economic development in the trans-Missouri West? Or was it a move to get the Kansas more involved in the overland trade, even if that involved alcohol?

Certainly there was no lack of evidence that improvement for the Kansas was in order, for in the wake of the 1825 treaty their quality of life diminished dramatically. Efforts to engage in agriculture failed miserably, as did educational promises under the

The interior of a saloon in Santa Fe about the time H. M. T. Powell, an English-born shopkeeper, visited there in 1852. Powell described Santa Fe as "a miserable hole, gambling and drinking in all directions." Courtesy of David Dary.

treaty. In 1827, while collecting their annuity near the overland road at Westport, a fatal malady—either cholera or smallpox—struck the tribe. Agent John Dougherty put the immediate number of dead at seventy; Superintendent William Clark reported the number at 180.[26]

Four years later, government surveyor Isaac McCoy advised the secretary of war that in view of their deplorable condition the Kansas should be relocated to some point west of the junction of the Smoky Hill and Republican Rivers, which would place them some 50 miles north of the overland road, and a decade later an eastern businessman whose primary interests were land speculation

"The Stage." Passing time on a stage express crossing Indian Country in 1861. From Harper's New Monthly Magazine *22 (1861): 152.*

informed Secretary of War James M. Porter that the Kansas were ready to sell their lands west of present day Topeka, as this would separate them from Missouri whiskey traders.[27] And not long thereafter, an Indian agent at Fort Leavenworth opined to St. Louis Superintendent William Harvey that back in 1825 William Clark had swung a "bad bargain" with the Kansas and that the best way to indemnify them would be a "liberal purchase of their remaining lands," which totaled 2 million acres.[28]

For their part the Kansas were well aware that annuities under the 1825 treaty would end in 1846; if not renewed, it would be impossible for them to make semiannual hunting expeditions to the western buffalo country and thereby continue to partake in the overland alcohol trade. As a result they were agreeable to ceding most of their lands in return for renewed annuity payments and a permanent reservation allowing them to live a secure life in a place at or near where their relatives had resided for generations and were now buried. The Mission Creek Treaty dated January 14, 1846, negotiated at the Methodist Kansas Mission west of present Topeka, did provide the tribe with renewed annuity payments and a so-called permanent home—but at a heavy cost to the tribe. For $202,000 with 5 percent interest for thirty years (slightly more than ten cents per acre), the tribe ceded all of the 2 million acres understood to be their exclusive tribal domain by the U.S. government twenty-one years earlier. The remaining issue was where the new reservation would be located. In this regard Article 3 of the treaty authorized a survey to determine the western limits of the ceded land, which turned out to be at or near the 98th Meridian in the lower Smoky Hill drainage some 50 miles north of the overland road. Article 4 required that in the event the new reservation would be lacking in timber the president of the United States would select a "more suitable" location. And assuming that the Kansas might be "exposed to difficulties with other tribes," they were promised a resident subagent for protection and other unspecified needs.[29]

As it turned out, the area near the 98th Meridian was indeed deficient in timber. Even though the location placed the Kansas closer to bison country and more distant from a regular supply of alcohol, it also placed them closer to Pawnee and Cheyenne enemies. Furthermore, it was reported that an unfriendly Comanche party had only recently been seen hunting in the same area. Ultimately, and with virtually no input from the Kansas except their preference for a site on the upper Neosho, it was Indian Commissioner William Medill in Washington and Superintendent Harvey in St. Louis who arbitrarily determined that the reservation would be no larger than 20 miles square.[30] And it was Kansa Agent Richard Cummins who actually selected what thereafter was called the Council Grove Kansas Reservation, with its boundaries

> To commence at a point ten miles due north of the Trading house of Boon [*sic*] and Hamilton[31] and the Government blacksmith shop, both of which are on the bank of council grove creek at the [Neosho] *crossing of the santifee road* [emphasis added], from thence due west five miles to corner, thence due south twenty miles, thence east twenty mile to corner, thence due north twenty miles to corner, thence due west fifteen miles to the place of beginning.[32]

In short, following more than two decades of misery with alcohol, the supposedly final homes for the Kansas were to be established alongside the overland road to New Mexico—the very road most traveled by alcohol traders on their way to bartering their commodities in Indian Country. What better vindication of Senator Benton's assertion: Where roads were established Indians were sure to follow.

7

On the Upper Arkansas

The Kansas were reluctant to take up residence on their new reservation, even though their 1846 treaty stipulated a May 1847 deadline for moving to Council Grove. They spent the winter of 1847–1848 begging from the military stores at Fort Leavenworth and from emigrant tribes. By the time they finally arrived at Council Grove in the spring of 1848 they were living on a "$3 per capita" emergency fund provided by the Indian Office in Washington. By then their agent had been advised that a new federal law had gone into effect (on March 3, 1847); for the first time ever, prison sentences up to two years could be imposed on persons convicted of "selling, exchanging, bartering, giving, or disposing of any spirituous liquor or wine to an Indian, in the Indian country." In response, Agent Richard Cummins informed his superiors in St. Louis regarding how traders, as they crossed over the new Kansa reservation at Council Grove, were disrupting the affairs of his agency; that large consignments of "spirituous liquors" had already been delivered into Indian Country; and many traders were planning to expand alcohol operations over the road to Santa Fe the following year.[1]

Clearly they were, apparently with little or no fear of arrest. At Council Grove and east to the Missouri border, at the Great Bend of the Arkansas, and west along the upper Arkansas as far as present Pueblo, Colorado, by the early 1840s most Plains Indians were being urged to trade bison robes for alcohol. It should be noted that even before the 1847 law went into effect the Indian Office in Washington was informed that the Shawnees and certain other emigrant tribes were "desirous for the government to give them a law [regarding alcohol] and have it executed." This was much easier said than done. One of his predecessors, said Agent Cummins, "had presented many of these [overland road] whiskey traders to a grand jury [in western Missouri] but they always managed to screen themselves and not one has been found guilty."[2]

Far to the west, in the upper Arkansas country, were the villages and hunting grounds of Comanches, Kiowas, Plains Apaches, Arapahoes, and Cheyennes—the latter an Algonquian-speaking people known as the Southern Cheyennes, in contrast to northern bands who preferred the Powder River and Laramie country of east-central Wyoming. A crude map attributed to Louis Jolliet, dated sometime prior to 1673, placed the original Cheyenne peoples ("Chaiens" on the map) not far above the mouth of the Wisconsin River. A century and a half later, following sojourns to present North Dakota, the Black Hills, and eastern Wyoming, Southern Cheyenne villages began to appear in the South Platte Basin in present northeastern Colorado; in the meantime their economy evolved from a mix of fishing, garden horticulture, and hunting to more hunting and trade contacts involving processed bison robes, horses, mules, and iron products.[3] Items that helped inspire a "great burst of power"[4] to

Close-up of contemporary bison grazing. Author J. Schmidt. Dated 1977. Wikimedia Commons.

Southern Cheyennes in the early nineteenth century were firearms and ammunition, courtesy of the British and French who, unlike the Spanish, had few qualms about arming Indians in pursuit of their own economic and diplomatic goals. Clearly, the Southern Cheyennes adjusted to gun technology with ease and took great pride in how this new technology improved their hunting capability and helped stabilize their population at roughly 3,000 persons, including some 900 warriors, to as late as 1855.[5]

And then there was alcohol, a controversial commodity that by the early 1830s was in ample supply on or near the overland roads to Taos and Santa Fe. Some accounts state that, on the upper Arkansas near present Pueblo and the mountain route of the overland road in 1832, the Southern Cheyennes first tasted alcohol. This came compliments of an unscrupulous American trader named John Gantt, who allegedly sweetened some whiskey to obtain furs and bison robes at bargain rates.[6] On this point, however, one version of the incident is less certain, stating that Gantt "*supposedly* [emphasis added] enticed the Cheyennes to drink alcohol sweetened with sugar and so turned them into a nation of drunkards. But it is hard to believe the Cheyennes had not already been introduced to liquor by other American and Mexican traders."[7] This seems possible; by then the Taos and Arroyo Hondo distilleries were up and running, as were counterparts in western Missouri, allowing traders from both the United States and Mexico with ample supplies to ply the liquid commodity all along Senator Benton's road. The Cheyenne people's migratory interlude in the upper Powder River and Black Hills country occurred prior to Gantt's supposed indiscretion. It was a trade region where the powerful American Fur Company was dominant well into the third decade of the nineteenth century. So it is plausible that at least some Cheyenne hunters had sampled that company's alcohol well before the tribe's migration south to the upper Arkansas. In 1832, from his post in central South Dakota, Upper Missouri Agent Jonathan Bean described the conditions supportive of that view:

> Liquor flows as freely here as the Missouri river, if we might judge the number of drunken Indians, yet no one gives them a drop, or at least, no proof can be had. For God's sake, for the sake of humanity, exert your yourself to have this article stopped in this country. . . . If I can place any confidence in the effort of the half Breeds and Indians, 2,200 Packs of Buffalo Robes have been purchased this year for whiskey at from 24 to 34 dollars per gallon.[8]

Assuredly there were a number of Southern Cheyennes in the upper Arkansas by the early 1820s. In late November 1821, the Jacob Fowler party, en route from Fort Smith, Arkansas, to the southern Rockies, observed at least two hundred Southern Cheyenne lodges on the southern bank of the Arkansas, some 75 miles east of present Pueblo, Colorado. Wrote Fowler, who also reported the encampments of several other Indian tribes in the vicinity:

> We have Heare now about seven Hundred lodges of the nations mentioned [Kiowas, Comanches, and Arapahoes] on [November] 25—With the addicion [addition] of the Cheans [Cheyennes] about two Hundred lodges—We suppose those Lodges to Contain from twelve to twenty pursons [persons] of all Sises [sizes]—Some Horses have been Stollen [stolen] Every night Since We [arrived] amongst them, seven of our own amongst the missing.[9]

Apparently the Cheyennes were on an extended hunting and raiding expedition for horses in an area better supplied with such animals than on the northern and central Plains. One factor may have been the Cheyennes' desire to maintain a greater number of horses for more systematic hunting, a response to the market in bison products expanding dramatically at that time.[10]

Alternatively, tribal ceremonialism and certain trade networks gave rise to fictive relationships and increased intertribal cooperation, primarily to assure the availability of food in times of famine. Grounded in archaeological and ethnohistorical evidence, this theory suggests that during the Pacific Climatic Episode (approximately 1200–1550 A.D.), when widespread drought was a threat to the available food supply, an indeterminate number of Great Plains people responded by locating their primary villages long distances from other tribes as a means of safeguarding trade partners from the same drought. This, then, may have been a factor in the southern movement of Cheyennes that Fowler encountered on the upper Arkansas in 1821, less than a month after William Becknell and his Missourians had traveled along the same river en route to the markets of northern New Mexico.[11]

In any case, it is evident that most of the more affluent and high-volume traders welcomed the Southern Cheyennes' move from eastern Wyoming and the Black Hills country to the upper Arkansas Basin and the area between the mouth of the Purgatoire and Big Timbers rivers, less than a day's travel from the overland roads to New Mexico.[12] Also, the more experienced upper Arkansas traders were well informed of significant changes then taking place in the Indian trade.

In the 1820s and early 1830s changing fashion tastes led to demand for silk hats; the price of beaver pelts (a major source of felt) decreased nearly 50 percent on the St. Louis and Chicago markets.[13] This change and the surging popularity of various forms of bison apparel, blankets, and rugs contributed to a dramatic increase in the market for bison robes and other bison products. This turn of events did not go unnoticed by Charles and William Bent, two young St. Louis traders who by the early 1830s were becoming well known for their interest in, as well as knowledge of, the overland trade with Mexico. Their father was Silas Bent, a prominent citizen of Massachusetts who served as a deputy surveyor for the Louisiana Territory prior to his arrival in St. Louis. There, in 1806, he was appointed a justice of the Court of Common Pleas, and in 1807 he became a judge of the Supreme Court of Louisiana Territory. Well connected in St. Louis social and political life, the large Bent family

William Bent. Courtesy of David Dary.

(Charles and William had five siblings) resided on a commanding bluff overlooking the Mississippi, with a sizable farm, a rambling two-story house, large barn, and adjoining sheds.[14] In St. Louis—by then the fur trade capital of the United States—the Bent brothers were attracted to the fur trade of the High Plains and Southwest. To them the changing character of the fur trade was a strong indicator that a good deal of money could be made by traders prepared and able to adjust to the new dispensation.

A reminiscence written by William Bent's son George, claiming that his father had worked for the American Fur Company in upper Missouri country as early as 1816,[15] is more fanciful than true; William would have been only seven years old at that time. Less debatable is that in 1827 he and his older brother Charles signed on with what turned out to be the Missouri Fur Trade Company's disastrous and unprofitable trapping and trading expedition to the

Charles Bent. Author not listed. Date not listed. Courtesy Wikimedia Commons.

Green River country of southwestern Wyoming. Wiser, but still full of ambition, the two invested in (apparently with family financial assistance) and bound themselves to a caravan of independent traders at Round Grove, Missouri, headed for Santa Fe in the spring of 1829.[16] Here, some 40 miles east of Westport at the mouth of the Kansas River, wagons were loaded with domestic cottons, silk, velvet, powder, lead, cookware, and hardware; whether they carried alcohol or whether they traded with Indians along the way is not known. Upon returning to St. Louis that fall it was announced that the caravan (including the Bent brothers' merchandise) had secured some $200,000 worth of bullion, animals, and goods—a very substantial profit from their investment a few months earlier. The following year Charles Bent went to Santa Fe with a larger caravan, this time with as many as sixty wagons and well over a hundred men.[17]

With him was Ceran St. Vrain, a St. Louis childhood friend who had been involved in the Santa Fe trade as early as 1824. He had clerked for the western department of the American Fur Company and, with Charles and brother William, founded Bent, St. Vrain & Co. in 1831. A important asset to the company's plan to engage in the Indian trade on the Taos and Santa Fe roads was St. Vain's marriage to a Mexican woman, which required baptism in the Catholic Church and led to his Mexican citizenship—a requirement for all individuals who wished to engage in the Indian trade. He also opened a store in Taos (with plans for another in Santa Fe); in the meantime, the Bent brothers focused on the upper Arkansas bison trade.[18]

While Charles Bent took on the administrative and more technical operations of Bent, St. Vrain & Co. that sometimes took him from the upper Arkansas to Westport and St. Louis, back to Taos and Santa Fe, and finally back to Westport during one season alone, William focused on regional operations and personal relations with Indians in the upper Arkansas. In 1830 or 1831, for example, he and his employees constructed a picket "headquarters" stockade on the northern side of the Arkansas a few miles below the mouth of Fountain Creek, near the site of modern Pueblo, Colorado. Here goods could be stored and traded to the Plains Indians, especially Southern Cheyennes and Arapahoes and, hopefully, Kiowas and Comanches as well.[19]

A major milestone for the fledgling company was reached on November 10, 1832, when the *Missouri Intelligencer* in Columbia announced that Charles Bent had just returned from Santa Fe with a "very considerable" amount of coin, bullion, mules, furs, and bison robes, amounting to an impressive $190,000 in value—evidence that the demand for bison robes was real and likely to increase. In fact, Charles was so impressed with his company's profit that he quickly invested $40,000 in goods for a return trip to Santa Fe.[20] Such news, of course, was welcome to his brother, then struggling to boost trade with the Southern Cheyennes at Fountain Creek. Fortunately, conditions there had improved considerably in late 1829 and early 1830,[21] when Chief Yellow Wolf of the Hairy Rope Band and a body of his warriors, while returning from a horse-raiding expedition against Bull Hump's band of Comanches in the Red River country south of the Arkansas, decided to visit Bent's new commercial facility at Fountain Creek. Chief Yellow Wolf and his warriors spent several days visiting and trading before heading north to their village on the South Platte, but without two straggling members of their party who found it necessary to hide on the stockade premises at Fountain Creek when Bull Hump and his warriors unexpectedly arrived on the scene, demanding to know if the two Cheyenne horse raiders were on the grounds or in the general vicinity. With resolve and no hint of equivocation, William Bent responded in the negative; after a short but tense pause, Buffalo Hump and his men departed and the lives of the two Cheyennes (and perhaps Bent himself) were saved. It was an incident of major importance, for it marked the beginning of William Bent's friendship and long association with the Southern Cheyennes, including his marriage to Owl Woman, daughter of White Thunder, Arrow Keeper of the tribe.[22]

By the early 1830s, Yellow Wolf and fellow leaders Little Wolf and Wolf Chief agreed to move their villages south in order to obtain more rewarding returns from the massive southern bison herd. They savored the benefits of a well-stocked trade center within easy travel of their newly located villages on the upper Arkansas. Completed in 1834 and initially known as Fort William, Bent's Fort was a large, citadel-like adobe structure located on the northern bank of the Arkansas less than a day's travel west of Big Timbers and only a few miles above the mouth of the Purgatoire River. This location was well within the range of Southern Cheyenne bison hunters and foretold the tribe's emerging economic power on the Southern Plains.[23]

But the imposing structure may not have been built primarily to accommodate Southern Cheyennes. In October 1831, Indian Superintendent William Clark in St. Louis was informed that the Arapahoes "inhabit the country from the Santa Fe trail to the headwaters of the Platte . . . [and] harass the Santa Fe traders and those engaged in the fur trade."[24] So did the Kiowas, Comanches, and bands of Apaches, he was told. In fact, the enmity and thievery of these Indians against the overland traders *and* the Southern Cheyennes may have been an important inducement for the Southern Cheyennes to relocate their villages near Bent's Fort. But for the spending of non-Indian vendors and merchants, and U.S. government personnel who traveled the Taos and Santa Fe roads, it seems doubtful that the Bents would have erected their grandiose emporium on the Arkansas.

Here for barter and purchase were customary Indian items such as beads, hawk bells, looking glasses, guns and powder, tobacco, blankets, axes, kettles, hoop iron, sugar, coffee, and, of course, liquor of all kinds (including "Pass Brandy, rum and Taos Lightening"). The Bents' inventory might also have included ropes, saddles, fringed Spanish shawls, bottles of pepper sauce, salt pork in barrels, horseshoes, kegs of blackstrap molasses, spare parts for wagons, boxes of water crackers, bags of flour, twists of brown chewing tobacco, ox shoes, bear traps, and bales of bison robes (i.e., articles that were more popular with non-Indians).[25] In short, Bent's Fort on Benton's road attracted Indians and non-Indians to the upper Arkansas, much like Council Grove did along the Neosho in the late 1840s and early 1850s. In fact, Benton's road induced important changes—most of them negative—in the economic stability and physical well-being of Indians. In this, no commodity was more overpowering than illegal, distilled alcohol. Osages, Kansas, Shawnees, Potawatomis, Delawares, Sacs and Foxes, and Ottawas were affected in the region between Council Grove and the mouth of the Kansas. So were Southern Cheyennes and Arapahoes, Kiowas, Comanches, and Plains Apaches who later hunted and camped in the upper Arkansas hinterland of Bent's Fort.

By the early 1830s, what seemed like a viable mix of national road development and traders' enterprise in the cause of Indian progress encountered a serious snag. Back in 1825, Benton and his associates had assumed that the land over which their road threaded westward was little more than a trifling part of the ever-expanding land base of the United States. This dated back to 1803 (when the Louisiana Purchase from France was negotiated) and more recently to 1821 (when the Adams-Onis Treaty with Spain was ratified by the Senate).

In the meantime the federal government negotiated numerous land treaties with Indian nations east of the western boundary of

Missouri, sometimes composed in excessive or roundabout detail, authorizing specific land to be ceded to the federal government by an Indian nation. This practice, which continued until terminated by Congress in 1873, led to repeated land cessions, with the remaining (or "unceded") land described simply as "Indian country." In time the negotiation of more and more cession treaties made it increasingly difficult to describe one place in relation to another within ever-decreasing spaces.

Congress finally addressed the problem in 1834 ("An Act to regulate trade and intercourse with the Indian tribes, and to preserve peace on the frontier").[26] Section 1 provided a more precise and presumably understandable definition of the boundaries of Indian Country. As it turned out, Council Grove was well within these boundaries, as was the confluence of the Missouri and Kansas Rivers, the Great Bend of the Arkansas, and Bent's Fort on the distant American side of the upper Arkansas. For at least some of the traders, certainly the more dedicated advocates of an unregulated and essentially market-driven approach to the overland trade, several sections of the 1834 law were irritating and objectionable.

In the early 1820s Senator Benton had been one of the more outspoken public figures ridiculing the government's overreaching factory system of Indian trade.[27] Now, in 1834, judicial authority, stricter requirements for licensing traders, and sanctions against the use of alcohol as a trade item with Indians were enforceable on the very road Benton had promoted and made national in name as well as reach. It appeared to hark back to the pre-1822 years, when too many federal regulations had stifled the "natural growth" of the Indian trade. At this point it was doubtful that the new law would be enforced and that it might fall victim to forces similar to those that had destroyed the Indian factory system in 1822.

8

Tribal Annuities and Bison Robes

Following a treaty in 1832 requiring the Kickapoo nation to cede its lands in Missouri in return for lands west of Missouri, not far north of the eastern terminus of the roads to Taos and Santa Fe, a tribal spokesman informed Special Commissioner E. A. Ellsworth that "we are afraid of the wicked water [alcohol] brought to us by our white friends. We wish to get out of its reach by land or water."[1] Commissioner Ellsworth's response was that the wicked water had already been carried 200 miles west of Missouri and that their Great Father in Washington was very sorry to learn this. But he would stop it by sending out judges to try the culprits and punish them for their wicked deeds.[2] In fact, by section 24 of the soon-to-be-passed Indian Trade and Intercourse Act of 1834, all matters for its implementation, including regulations regarding alcohol in Indian Country, were assigned to the judicial districts of Missouri and Arkansas Territory. Usually these were hundreds of miles from where the actual violations might have taken place,[3] thus rendering Ellsworth's assurances to the Kickapoo people problematic at best.

In a letter to Secretary of War Lewis Cass in 1831, St. Louis Indian Superintendent William Clark forcefully recommended the "total and entire prohibition" of alcohol in Indian Country, followed by the reasons why violators were almost never prosecuted. The accuser who instituted a suit against the trader's bond, said Clark, would soon find what a difficult and complex matter he had undertaken. It would prove nothing that he had actually witnessed the practice of reducing the alcohol in the trader's house and pouring it into casks for delivery and sale to the Indians. He would have to prove that he had in fact tasted this liquor and found it to be spirituous in order to secure a conviction—an act in and of itself perilous to his own legal well-being in the eyes of the law.[4]

While laws to monitor the use and production of alcohol in Indian Country prior to 1834 were lax and minimally punitive, the trend by the early 1820s indicated a tightening up, a movement toward total prohibition, and more severe sentences for convicted violators. The operating (and obviously racist) assumption underlying these measures was that native peoples were at a rudimentary stage in their progression toward "civilized" life and thus vulnerable to the ingestion of alcohol.[5] Even Lewis Cass, well informed on American Indians and their culture,[6] observed in 1827 that "elsewhere habitual drunkards have paroxysms of intoxication followed by sobriety, but as long as the stimulus [alcohol] can be obtained, an Indian abandons himself totally to its indulgence, with the recklessness of desperation."[7] English scientist George W. Featherstonhaugh agreed. Given their "inordinate passion" for alcohol, he concluded, "the Indians appeared to have no other ambition than that of passing through life in a perpetual state of delirium."[8] Even so, the government's efforts to save the Indians by prohibiting alcohol in their own country was gradual, not least because of the enormous profits that could be gained from trading that commodity with Indians there.

An amendment to the Trade and Intercourse Act of 1802 for the first time gave the president of the United States authority to prevent and restrain the vending and distribution of spirituous liquors among "all or any of said Indian tribes" but with no specific penalty provided for violators.[9] What followed were a few trifling territorial laws, mainly in the Old Northwest, authorizing fines and/or prison terms for traders found guilty of selling alcohol to Indians. Many violations were often ignored or inadequately litigated in the frontier courts of a hard-drinking white population; adult ingestion of alcohol in 1830 averaged more than seven gallons per year.[10]

In 1815 the federal government gingerly moved forward with a law declaring that the operation of distilleries in Indian Country was illegal—but with no provisions for enforcement or sanctions for violators.[11] In 1822 another amendment to the Indian Trade and Intercourse Act of 1802 simply increased the bonds of licensed traders to $5,000 and directed Indian agents, subagents, superintendents, and military personnel "to cause" the stores and packages of goods of all traders to be searched, "upon suspicion or information that ardent spirits [were being] carried into the Indian countries by said traders." If found, all of the nefarious commodity was to be forfeited, half to the informant and half to the government, with the offender's license being revoked and his bond placed in suit.[12]

Certainly by the time William Becknell had demonstrated the value of overland trade between Missouri and New Mexico, and the factory system of Indian trade had been terminated, the federal government was increasingly concerned regarding the possibly destructive impact that unregulated alcohol might have on Indians.

Copy of "A Pack Train to Santa Fe in 1820." Artist Frederic Remington's drawing of one form of overland commercial transport from Missouri to Taos, Santa Fe, and points between, in Colonel Henry Inman, The Old Santa Fe Trail *(1897). Courtesy of David Dary.*

Thus it authorized the first genuine Indian prohibition law on July 9, 1832, which in plain terms stated that "no ardent spirits shall be hereafter introduced, under any pretense, into the Indian country."[13] No new penalties were authorized by the law, however. A new definition of Indian Country was provided by Congress two years later, clarifying the far western extent of that vast region.

The problem of enforcement continued and was made more challenging by the vast expanse of the trans-Missouri West. Also there was mounting competition between small-time alcohol peddlers and large companies such as Bent, St. Vrain & Co. and the American Fur Company. An agitated complaint to the St. Louis

Indian Office in 1842 by an American Fur Company official—representing a firm that could depend on the support of Senator Benton on most matters relating to alcohol, profits, and the Indian trade[14]—illustrates well a particularly onerous aspect of enforcement:

> Contrary to our well founded expectation, the government as yet has taken no measures to prevent this violation of the laws in regard to the introduction of liquor in Indian Country. . . . But if no steps are taken and the [Indian] Country is left open to every peddler and licensed trader to take what amount of liquor he pleases, we will be compelled in self-deference to pursue the excuse we may view as best calculated to protect us in trade from our opponents.[15]

These were strong, well-chosen words, indicating that the stakes were high for those dealing, or contemplating dealing, alcohol to Indians and hoping that the profits would be commensurate with the risks involved. Easy access to tribal camps, villages, and reservations was made possible by Senator Benton's well-marked and freely accessible road through the Indian Country. But beyond that were developments no less supportive of the alcohol business along the overland road to Mexico.

One was a result of the government's removal policy in the trans-Missouri West that began in 1825 and continued for more than two decades, resulting in the removal of some 10,000 midwestern Indians to the area between the mouth of the Kansas River and Council Grove. Like the Trail of Tears experienced by the Five Civilized Tribes from the Southeast to future Oklahoma, anguish and suffering resulted from these removals. To lessen the anticipated cultural shock, most of the removal treaties provided annuities to assist the emigrant tribes in adjusting to their new environment and living conditions. Added to these annuities, which over time aggregated to many thousands of dollars, were $150,000 in annuities issued in 1825 to the "resident" Osages and Kansas, mainly to compensate them for land soon to be occupied by the removal Indians.

One nineteenth-century study dealing with the impacts of removal upon local and regional economic development concluded that the total payments to the removal Indian nations west of Missouri alone—including some who had signed treaties predating the removal treaties—came to more than $1 million per year.[16] Importantly, most of the new removal reservations were not much more than 50 miles from Senator Benton's road, and some were much closer than that.

The Miamis, for example, whom the government placed south of the Kansas river on the western Missouri boundary less than a day's travel from the overland road, were awarded a total government payment of $885,000 under the treaties of 1838 and 1840, to be paid in ten and twenty annual payments.[17] Likewise, the federal obligation to the nearby Shawnees, whose reservation was actually traversed by the road to New Mexico, came to nearly that much. Thousands of additional federal dollars were paid annually to the Ottawas, Delawares, Potawatomis, Sacs and Foxes of Mississippi, Kickapoos, Kansas, Osages, Peorias, Kaskaskias, Weas, and Piankashaws.[18] Indeed, the payment of so many dollars to so many displaced people, in an unfamiliar but concentrated area, was an alcohol trader's dream.

Reports regarding alcohol taken into Indian Country are scanty and difficult to find, for the obvious reason that illegal transactions as a general rule do not appear on company ledgers or in individual or company promotional releases provided to the local or regional press. What is available, however, can be telling.

One report initially became newsworthy more because of the weather and agricultural conditions it reported than for the overland alcohol business. Due to drought and the consequent failure of the corn crop in western Missouri in 1827, merchants James and Robert Aull of Lexington and Independence, Missouri, purchased more than 700 gallons of whiskey from an Ohio wholesaler, which the Aulls reported was "for the Santa Fe trade."[19] In 1841, while traveling west with a Santa Fe caravan, Ohio journalist and political activist Rufus B. Sage discovered that the caravan he was traveling with was carrying a large consignment of alcohol—some twenty-four barrels at least—specifically "designed for the Indian trade."[20] The following year, Indian officials in Washington were advised that "whenever money is around [in Indian Country] it soon finds its way into the hands of the whiskey dealers, who swarm like birds of evil omen around the place where annuities are paid."[21] That same year, Baptist missionary and government surveyor Isaac McCoy reported that at least 30,000 gallons of whiskey were annually being transported into Indian Country,[22] and in 1848 Indian Superintendent David Mitchell in St. Louis was informed that most of the trade that year for Santa Fe would be in "spirituous liquors."[23] On the Council Grove reservation a few years later it was reported that the Indian alcohol laws were "openly flaunted" by traders who kept the Kansas well supplied with whiskey that, according to local white community leaders, "provoked" the Kansas to molest and steal from the Santa Fe wagon trains on a regular basis.[24]

Also at Council Grove a newspaper reported in 1859 that the entire Kansa tribe was drunk following the regular distribution of their annuities.[25] And Indian Commissioner T. Hartley Crawford's

"Prairie Schooners." Illustration of an overland wagon train, in B. Kroupa An Artist's Tour: Gleamings and Impressions of Travels in North and Central America and the Sandwich Islands *(London: Ward and Downey, 1890), courtesy of Denver Public Library, Western History Collections.*

1838 reported on the Sacs and Foxes of Mississippi, whose northern reservation boundary was only a few miles south of the overland road, less than a day's travel from Council Grove and the alcohol vendors there: Quoting the Sac and Fox agent, Commissioner Crawford deplored the fact "that the whole of the two nations have done little else [over the past year] than live upon the presents of horses &cc. given them, drink whiskey, and live among the white settlers on their borders in their own [Indian] country." Likewise, on the Potawatomi reservation not far north of Council Grove, it was reported by Lieutenant Colonel John Charles Frémont in 1853 that little was going on there except men of the tribe lounging about while consuming "lots of John Barleycorn."[26]

An especially dismal summary was a report from Superintendent David D. Mitchell to the Indian commissioner in 1843. Because the whiskey dealers were never found around the "poorer" (i.e., nonannuity) tribes, wrote Mitchell, more benevolent policy should be directed toward the payment of annuities in the form of merchandise that were attendant to individual Indians needs, not that of tribal leaders. Angrily, Mitchell castigated the "worthless characters" who were marrying Indian women with "the sole view of getting distributive shares [of the annuity fund]." The only interest of these detestable mortals was to keep the whiskey flowing, "which caused death among the tribes and a consequent increase in the annuity share of each member."[27]

In this context it is important to remember that Indian people in the upper Arkansas country were unable to partake in the annuities-for-alcohol system monetarily until 1851, when the Treaty of Fort Laramie inaugurated the distribution of annuities to several of the Plains tribes, including the Cheyennes and Arapahoes, and to the Kiowas, Comanches, and Plains Apaches at Fort Atkinson after 1853.[28] In the meantime, individual outlets for alcohol cropped up along the roads to Taos and Santa Fe. "Traveling groceries," as the business operations of many itinerant alcohol traders were called, became the source of frequent complaints by Indian agents and the military. A report from the Fort Leavenworth Agency in 1847 recounted how "retailers of [spirituous] liquors on the road" were banding with established caravans heading from western Missouri to the upper Arkansas to gain 100 or more safe miles into Indian Country.[29] This happened in the summer of 1846 near Plumb Creek, a few miles west of the Great Bend of the Arkansas. Here a detachment of Missouri volunteers heading for Santa Fe encountered a trader who sold them whiskey at exorbitant prices, "$1 per pint for 18 cents whiskey."[30]

Strong competition for the traveling groceries were the so-called stops or stations along the road between Westport and the mouth of Pawnee Fork, a landmark creek emptying into the Arkansas some 20 miles southwest of Great Bend. At 110 Mile Crossing, a day's journey from Westport and not far from the Sac and Fox reservation, was a stop operated by Fry McGee of the prominent James Hyatt McGee family of Westport—one of the most notorious alcohol dealers in Indian Country. At Lost Springs, on the overland road 100 miles west of McGee's, was a combination hotel and tavern where, on one occasion, the proprietor Thomas Wise was trapped on the roof of his establishment for half a day by unidentified Indians who demanded whiskey. A day's travel farther west to Cottonwood Crossing, "Red Jacket Bitters, Hostetters, Ginger Brandy, cognac, sweet wine, and whiskey galore" were available for anyone (including Indians) with cash or market-quality trade goods. Still farther west, at Cow Creek Crossing in present Rice County, Kansas, Asabel Beach and his son Abijah operated a territorial-chartered toll bridge, post office, and store specializing in sugar, coffee, bacon, flour, and whiskey. Beyond that, at Walnut Creek Crossing near present Great Bend, was the notorious "whiskey ranch" established in the 1840s by William Allison of Independence, Missouri, which under subsequent operators became one of the principal sources of alcohol for the southern Plains tribes.[31]

West of Pawnee Fork, stops on the road were less frequent for several reasons: the opening of alternative routes such as the Upper and Lower Cimmaron, the Aubury cutoff, and the Fort Union/Granada Cutoff; less traffic, as unseasoned travelers returned to Missouri; fewer tribes with annuity dollars to spend; and, after 1834, the increasing popularity of Bent's Fort on the upper Arkansas. Here, near the mouth of the Purgatoire in one of the more isolated areas of the overland roads, was a well-stocked emporium, a skillful wagon and harness service, ample forage for famished draft animals, and a regular supply of alcohol—all within a stone's thrown of the actual road. It also was a popular Indian trade center owned and operated by Charles and William Bent (and Ceran St. Vrain following organization of Bent, St. Vrain & Co. in 1830). As the largest buyer of Indian skins and robes on the upper Arkansas prior to the Mexican War, their business added credence to Senator Benton's insistence that roads and the commercial activity they generated were vital to the survival and improvement of the Indian race.

But the backstory—how the actual site was determined and how it became an almost immediate success—might have surprised even the expansionist Benton. For one thing, Charles and William had some trading experience with Indians prior to the construction of the Fort on the upper Arkansas—Charles on the Missouri with the Sioux, and William with unidentified Indians at the mouth of Fountain Creek near modern Pueblo, Colorado.[32] Later, in 1829, the brothers made a substantial profit with the Santa Fe caravan that was escorted to the international boundary by Major Bennet Riley and companies of the 6th Infantry. In St. Louis the Bents were a family of means, leading to view that Charles and William took money with them when they went west in the early 1820s. A decade later, Bent, St. Vrain & Co. had a store in Taos, another on the drawing board for Santa Fe, and trade goods and related assets valued at more that $100,000 dollars.[33]

The Bents were young, energetic, and venturesome—entrepreneurs of serious intent. Even so, Bent's Fort might not have gotten off to a profitable start without the help of certain Southern

Cheyenne leaders, according to anthropologist George Bird Grinnell, based on his interview with a prominent Cheyenne leader sometime prior to 1913. Wrote Grinnell in 1922, in an account repeated (with minor changes)[34] by several writers since:

> This old man [Porcupine Bull] asserted that the Bents and the Cheyennes first met at the mouth of the Purgatoire River. This was soon after the Cheyennes began moving south of the Platte, probably in 1828. The Bents were encamped at the mouth of the Purgatoire, or had a stockade there, and to this place came a party of Cheyennes who had been south catching horses. . . . Porcupine Bull stated that the leaders of this party were Yellow Wolf, Lone Wolf and Wolf Chief, and that it was at this meeting that Yellow Wolf made friends with the Bents. . . . The question of trade was also discussed, and Yellow Wolf told the Bents that a post on Arkansas near the mountains was too far from the buffalo range for the Indians to frequent. He suggested that the Bents and St. Vrain build a post near the mouth of the Purgatoire, and said if they would do this he would bring his band and others there to trade. . . . Charles Bent at once accepted the chief's proposal and this was how Bent's Fort came to be built.[35]

This may have been an oversimplification. A more recent study has emphasized that the Southern Cheyennes were on the upper Arkansas at least a decade before construction of Bent's Fort began in 1833 and that "the post was not established primarily to trade with the Cheyennes, since they were far less numerous [in that area] than the Arapahoes, Comanches, and Kiowas."[36] More likely, it was the establishment of Benton's "national" road leading to Taos

An unidentified artist made this drawing of a trading ranch at what became Lakin, Kansas Territory, on the Santa Fe road. The structure was a dugout made of sod cut from the ground. Courtesy of David Dary.

and Santa Fe, coupled with the increasing number of Indian people attracted to the upper Arkansas soon after the road was opened in 1821 that prompted the Bents to invest heavily in the trade center near the mouth of the Purgatoire. Charles Bent was elected captain of military-escorted caravans in 1829 and 1833[37] and had every reason to believe that Senator Benton would continue to pressure the Jackson administration for military assistance along the road.[38] In 1821, the Western Comanches would still organize and sponsor a trade fair at Big Timbers for some five hundred Cheyennes, Arapahoes, Kiowas, Plains Apaches, and Eastern Shoshones; by 1835, the Bent brothers at their "adobe castle" on the Arkansas were the preferred merchants and brokers of the Southern Plains.[39]

In August that same year, Orderly Sergeant Hugh Evans, of Colonel Henry Dodge's expedition to the Rocky Mountains, reported a large encampment of "Shyan" (Cheyenne) Indians near Bent's Fort, whose proprietors "traded extensively with the Indians, also with the Mexicans at Touse [Taos]" less than 100 miles away. Some of the more distinguished men and warriors of the Cheyennes "were out killing buffalo," wrote Evans in his journal,

> while the principal inmates [*sic*] of the town were women & children & old men. All (or nearly all) men, women and children were drunk and such a sight my eyes never before beheld. They were crowded in a large lodge . . . with a keg in the center and every one going as he [or she] felt disposed, filling their bowls and horn spoons and handing it about with as much liberality as a candidate for office. Some reeling, staggering and hollowing, falling down and raising up, frothing and foaming at the mouth perfectly insensible of what they were doing. . . . After remaining in their encampment for about two hours we came off sickened and disgusted at the site and returned to our encampment.[40]

Whether the Cheyennes had traded bison robes for their keg of alcohol Evans did not say; nor did he identify who the traders were. They may have been the Bents or one of their subordinates, or they might have been one or several of the independent operators. In any case, the alcohol most certainly came to the Cheyennes via the overland road, either from Missouri to the east or from Taos

This illustration by Frederic Remington may have been based on wagon-train travel over Raton Pass. Titled "An Ox Train in the Mountains," it appeared in Harper's Weekly, *May 26, 1888. Courtesy of David Dary.*

or Arroyo Hondo[41] by way of Pueblo and the Sangre de Cristo Pass to the west. Benton's road was emerging as a magnet for alcohol on the upper Arkansas in Indian Country, much like the Missouri River for years had served Indian Country to the northwest.[42]

One historian of the upper Arkansas has dismissed as "an absurd assertion" the belief that the Bents may not have used alcohol at all in the Indian trade.[43] And recent biographers of George Bent (son of William Bent and Owl Woman) have concluded that in fact the Bents began using alcohol as a trade item well before they began building their trade center near the Purgatoire.[44]

Alexander Barclay, who was the Bents' resident superintendent between 1838 and 1842, claimed that Bent, St. Vrain & Co. made an annual return of between $20,000 and $50,000 during that time span, mainly from bison robes. In the South Platte Valley where the Bents competed against the American Fur Company, the area "was soaked in illicit alcohol." Even the skins, viscera, and skeletal parts of the bison were measured for sale in barrels for whiskey, and on the basis of Barclay's reporting, it has been stated that "it is inconceivable that he [Barclay] and his friends did not themselves participate in the lucrative business."[45] Indian trader James Beckworth recalled that in the winter of 1839–1840 he carried forty gallons of whiskey on his wagon trip from the Arkansas to the South Platte, and that before half the whiskey had been traded he had obtained sixteen horses and over two hundred robes from the Indians.[46]

In response to the increasing quantity of illegal alcohol being taken into Indian Country, yet another federal law was passed in 1847, this time calling for larger fines than in the past and/or up to two years' imprisonment for convicted offenders. And for the first time Indians were allowed to serve as competent witnesses in federal courts dealing with alleged Indian Country alcohol traders.[47]

By the mid-1840s, then, life along the overland roads was different than it had been when William Becknell first traveled from Missouri to New Mexico two decades earlier. Bison hunting and processing had increased dramatically, Plains Indian encampments near the road were commonplace, the Bents' commercial center on the banks of the upper Arkansas was attracting more customers each year, Indian raiding for horses and mules from the wagon trains was increasing (especially in the area between Council Grove and the Great Bend of the Arkansas), and alcohol was more plentiful that ever in the Indian Country west of Missouri—federal law notwithstanding.

In the mid-1840s the movement of white Americans across the prairie-plains would more than double. Bickering over the border between the United States and Mexico intensified, calm and reason gave way to violence, and war with Mexico finally erupted in 1846. The burgeoning number of overland travelers over Benton's road were crossing into a complicated and economically volatile place called Indian Country. Indian peoples were being introduced to a market economy and alcohol by white traders in exchange for bison products the Indians harvested in their own country.

9

Trade Alcohol

Writing from his headquarters at Bent's Fort in 1855, Upper Arkansas Indian Agent John Whitfield reported to his superiors in St. Louis that the Cheyennes, numbering approximately 3,000 individuals, were killing perhaps 40,000 bison per year, more that twice the number required for their own subsistence, and leaving the rest to be processed for white traders, or left to rot. Whitfield's numbers may have been inflated, but even to process a 10 percent lesser number of animals each year would have required individual Cheyenne women to finish no less that one robe per week, suggesting that Cheyenne men were beginning to assist in the tasks traditionally performed by women.[1]

Processing bison robes for market was labor-intensive, requiring drying by staking the robe to the ground for several days and rubbing it repeatedly with macerated bison or elk brains to maintain the robe's flexibility. It also required scraping the meaty side to keep it resilient and then smoking it in a small lodgelike enclosure for several days to make it water-resistant. All of this pointed to a restricted annual production rate per individual Cheyenne woman, especially if it is remembered that these women had other duties to perform: child-rearing, food preparation, assembling and disassembling lodges, and managing pack animals to accommodate what then was evolving into as a more focused hunter-processing-trading culture.[2] Certainly as the market for robes expanded, Cheyenne men, who viewed themselves as hunters and warriors, took part—albeit reluctantly—in the mundane and less exciting tasks of preparing robes for market.

The fact that Southern Cheyennes and several bands of Arapahoes traded many hundreds of finished bison robes per year from their Big Timbers and Bent's Fort village in the 1830s and 1840s is indisputable. In fact, the market was growing dramatically. At St. Louis on December 13, 1834, Charles Bent (for Bent, St. Vrain & Co.) was issued a two-year federal license to trade (employing twenty-nine men) with "the Arapahoes, Cheyennes, Kiowas, Snakes, Sioux, and Arikaras" at several locations, including "Fort William [Bent's Fort], on the north side of the Arkansas about 40 miles [*sic*] east of the Rocky Mts."[3] Soon thereafter the company's trade with the Southern Cheyennes and Arapahoes grew dramatically. In the summer of 1839, for example, it was reported that Bent, St. Vrain & Co. shipped 600 packs or bales of robes (each bale containing twenty to thirty robes) to St. Louis. In 1840 the firm shipped 15,000 robes to the same market; 27,500 robes went to St. Louis in 1841; and the following year 4,000 robes were delivered to Westport by way of the overland road, with a reported 6,500 more held in storage at Bent's massive upper Arkansas facility—robes that would be shipped to Westport or St. Louis at a later date.[4]

In the meantime, a series of interrelated events in 1840 contributed to an increase in the bison robe trade along the upper

Arkansas. Dating back to the late eighteenth century the Cheyennes had enjoyed mostly peaceful relations with the Kiowas and Comanches, who ranged south of the Arkansas and west to the Sangre de Cristo Mountains and who, by the early 1830s, had worked out a alliance among themselves. But the increasingly popular practice of raiding for horses south of the Arkansas and in the upper Canadian Basin—for trade with neighboring tribes and white traders—led to a spirited competition between the Kiowas and Comanches on the one side and the Southern Cheyennes and Arapahoes on the other. Eventually this led to violence. In 1837, forty-two members of the Bowstring warrior society of the Cheyennes were killed while engaged in a horse-stealing raid against Kiowas on the upper Washita, in present western Oklahoma. The following year, a Cheyenne-Arapaho party rode against the Kiowas at Wolf Creek, some 80 miles northwest of the Washita battle site that left many dead on both sides. Mounting death rates across tribal lines encouraged settlement, which was achieved in the summer of 1840 on the Arkansas near Bent's Fort, where prominent leaders of both sides met with pledges of friendship and the exchange of gifts, some highly esteemed objects because of their "medicine."

A reportedly "calamitous disease" (possibly cholera) earlier that year afflicted several Plains tribes and may have encouraged the great peace of 1840, a collective response to intertribal suffering. At the same time, peace was urged by the Bents, who stood to benefit by having the Kiowas and Comanches hunt north of the Arkansas without fear of Cheyenne retaliation. Writing to Manuel Alvarez in Santa Fe in 1841, Charles Bent said that he expected no less than 1,500 Comanche lodges to be set up near his trade establishment; not long thereafter he reported that thirty-one Kiowa and

Comanche headmen had actually arrived at Bent's Fort. Clearly, the High Plains bison country between the Platte and the Arkansas had become a shared hunting ground of former adversaries at a time when the demand for bison robes was intensifying.

In a related matter that same year, on the western Missouri border 500 miles east of Bent's Fort, printer and journalist Rufus B. Sage was taken aback when in broad daylight he observed numerous barrels of alcohol being placed on wagons at Westport and Independence, awaiting the journey to Council Grove and west to the upper Arkansas. Two federal agents were stationed at Westport, said Sage, and six to eight companies of U.S. dragoons were stationed at nearby Fort Leavenworth—a force adequate to interdict the illegal shipments into Indian Country. "Yet the traffic suffered no diminution from their vigilance!" reported the much confounded Sage.[5]

It is possible, of course, that the barrels of alcohol observed by Sage were specifically consigned for non-Indian markets in Taos, Santa Fe, or other Mexican settlements farther south. But this is unlikely given the ample supply of alcohol produced by distilleries in the Taos and Santa Fe areas. In 1836, for example, distiller Simon Turley sent one of his most trusted employees to the upper Arkansas and South Platte to market flour and alcohol produced at his Arroyo Hondo distillery just north of Taos.[6] In 1840 former Bent, St. Vrain & Co. employee Jim Beckworth returned to the upper Arkansas from Taos with alcohol "for the Cheyenne trade,"[7] in competition with his former employers. As early as 1838 certain Mexican merchants were hauling merchandise that included alcohol to certain undesignated markets between Santa Fe and the mouth of the Kansas. And at the federal level, Indian Commissioner T. Hartley Crawford in Washington was informed in 1843

"Indians Hunting the Bison," by Karl Bodmer, in Maximilian zu Wied-Neuwied, Maximilian Prince of Wied's Travels in the Interior of North America, during the Years 1832–1834, *translated by H. Evans Lloyd, Achermann & Co., London 1843-1844. Wikimedia Commons.*

that "petty traders" from northern Mexico were bringing in a regular supply of alcohol for trading with Cheyennes in the upper Arkansas country, as well as with other bison hunters living there. "Could not this be prevented by negotiations with the British and Mexican ministers?" was one question posed by St. Louis Superintendent David D. Mitchell to the Indian Office in Washington.[8] This despite knowing full well that halting the flow of alcohol on the roads from western Missouri to the upper Rio Grande was a low priority, both in Washington and in Mexico. In fact, most Mexican merchants had little regard for Indian alcohol laws. When urged by their government to pay heed to northern neighbors, they refused to do so while protecting their own investments in the alcohol business by bribing the occasional Mexican official who tried to enforce the laws of the United States.[9]

Mexican disdain for the American law of 1832 requiring that "no ardent spirits shall hereafter be introduced, under any pretense, into the Indian Country" was essentially a pragmatic position acknowledging the enormous profits traders from either country could obtain from Indians so long as they were agreeable to alcohol as the preferred payment for bison robes. And it further implied that the 1832 law would be flaunted as long as the United States refused to provide the resources necessary for real enforcement, including prison sentences for convicted offenders. In the meantime, profits from the alcohol trade became staggering.

The official U.S. National Park Service tour guide for Bent's Old Fort[10] informs visitors today that bison hides purchased from Indians in the upper Arkansas country brought an average of 25 cents' value in "trade goods" that in turn were sold by white traders for $3 to $6 on the St. Louis and other eastern markets. Whether these goods included alcohol is not specified; neither is there any mention of Indians exchanging bison robes for alcohol in general. But that practice is beyond dispute.

Along the overland road southwest of Westport, the Sac and Fox government agent complained that whiskey valued at twenty cents per gallon in Leavenworth was sold for $5 per gallon to Indians, "and well watered at that."[11] Not far distant from Bent's Fort, trader James Beckworth reported in 1840 that "one pint of alcohol, costing no more than six cents [in Missouri], was manufactured into five times the quantity of whiskey, usually one pint for one buffalo robe,"[12] which brought ten dollars or more on the St. Louis market. In more recent times it has been determined that white traders paid the Southern Cheyennes $3 in alcohol for a robe that could bring up to $15 at Westport. The same study noted that, unlike metal goods, guns, ammunition, and bolts of cloth, alcohol, once consumed, was no burden for Indians to carry. Indians could use only a finite number of knives, guns, and metal utensils, while their demand for alcohol had no limit. Watered down and sometimes laced with red pepper or tobacco juice, a gallon of alcohol typically sold for $16, or five prime bison robes.[13] Additional statistics are available elsewhere, but for sheer poignancy the words of Edward Sabin seldom have been equaled:

> Let the reader sit down and figure up the profits of a forty-gallon keg of alcohol, and he will be thunderstruck or whiskey-struck. When disposed of, four gallons of water are added to each gallon of [raw] alcohol. In two hundred gallons there are sixteen hundred pints, for each of which the trader gets a buffalo robe worth five dollars. The Indian women toil many long weeks to dress sixteen hundred robes. . . . Six thousand dollars for sixty gallons of alcohol! Is it any wonder that, with such profits in prospect, men get rich who are engaged in the trade.[14]

Traders operating in the field were a varied lot. Some were individual operators who consigned only a limited number of robes to large firms such as Bent, St. Vrain & Co. at Bent's Fort; some were unnamed jobbers who frequented points along the overland road such as Walnut Creek Ranch near the Great Bend of the Arkansas,[15] Fort Larned near Pawnee Fork, and several wholesale houses at Council Grove.[16] The few who could afford a team of mules and a wagon might haul their bounty directly to Joseph S. Chick's warehouses at Westport or to other prominent jobbers operating out of Liberty or nearby Independence. But the bulk of the Indian bison trade prior to 1850 involved Bent, St. Vrain & Co. In 1839 the company employed nearly a hundred traders and trappers who, following a successful trip, "were jubilant and usually staid [*sic*] at the fort playing cards, drinking whiskey, and carousing till a new party would organize." Likewise, a Shawnee hunting party returning to their reservation near the mouth of the Kansas a few years later sold a large number of mules stolen from Mexicans south of Santa Fe at Bent's Fort and were "much delighted to receive so much gold for their animals, and, before they got away from fort, some of it was spent for choice brandies, wines, and whiskies, &c . . . and for several days there was much feasting and carousing."[17]

The Shawnees were not the only Indians to engage in the alcohol business in Indian Country. Like the Shawnees and other emigrant tribes near the overland road to Mexico, the Kansas exploited their strategic location at Council Grove to the utmost.

They apparently learned well that whatever else the white man's sanctions might mean regarding the use of trade alcohol for Indian commodities, those sanctions had no meaning and were thus of no interest to them. In fact, one might be tempted to conclude that insofar as alcohol was concerned, the Kansas displayed entrepreneurial talents bordering on that of William Bent hundreds of miles to the west. In 1835, William Bent married Owl Woman, daughter of Southern Cheyenne dignitary White Thunder, thereby becoming a legal member of the tribe. He was no longer hampered by the white man's rules regarding exchanging bison robes for alcohol.[18] Great Bend trader Charles Rath at Walnut Creek Ranch in 1860 married Roadmaker, a Southern Cheyenne woman, and divorced "Indian-style" three years later.[19] Whatever else one might

Fort Larned, near the overland road to New Mexico and the confluence of Pawnee Creek and the Arkansas, as sketched by Theodore R. Davis for Harper's Weekly, *June 8, 1867. Courtesy of Kansas State Historical Society.*

say about these wily businessmen (sometimes called "squawmen" in the post–Civil War years), the fact is they were well schooled in Indian culture, alcohol, and the profits that might accrue from harmonious tribal relationships, while at the same time evading federal Indian alcohol laws dating back to the days of Jackson. In fact, the federal Indian alcohol statute of 1874 finally conceded what these merchant traders had understood all along:

Every person, *except an Indian* [emphasis added], in the Indian country, who shall, sell, exchange, give, barter, or dispose of an spirituous liquor or wine to any Indian under the charge of any Indian superintendent or agent, or agent, or introduce or attempt to introduce any spirituous liquor into the Indian country, shall be punishable by imprisonment for not more than two years, and by a fine of not more than three hundred dollars.[20]

A number of Kansa tribesmen entered into the Indian alcohol trade between Missouri and Council Grove. In 1833 Kansa Agent

Marston G. Clark dispatched a strongly worded letter to Superintendent Clark in St. Louis, complaining of the huge quantities of whiskey the Kansas were obtaining from the overland traders near the mouth of the Kansas River, just across the line in Missouri. Much of this alcohol the Kansas took back to villages for personal consumption, but a good amount was traded with nearby emigrant tribes recently arrived from the East. "Having no force to prevent it," Agent Clark complained, "the Indians carry on the traffic with impunity."[21] That same year, Fort Leavenworth Indian Agent Richard Cummins communicated a similar message, this time directly to the Indian Office in Washington: "The evil does exist," wrote Cummins, "and it is ardent spirits that causes many of them to steal one from another, to kill one another in combats when drunk, [and] to neglect all kinds of business. . . . I am at a loss to know whether you intended that I should seize the article when found in the possession of the Indian."[22] By 1841 it was reported that most of the Kansa nation was consuming alcohol on a regular basis,[23] and in 1859 a local paper in Council Grove reported that the entire tribe was drunk following receipt of its annual government distribution.[24] The results were predictable: dwindling interest in hunting, stealing from the Taos and Santa Fe wagon trains, untended fields, sickness, and premature death. In 1862 the bodies of six murdered Kansa men were found near the "grocery" of Council Grove bootlegger J. L. French, located within a stone's throw of the Santa Fe road. An earlier report stated that a large distillery was under construction "on the Santa Fe Trail between the Missouri River and Council Grove."[25] Demographically, the news was no less disheartening. In 1858, the tribal population was 1,037, "200 less than the previous year." Four years later the number was 802, and a decade later it was down to 700—with not one male over the age of fifty-five.[26] Collectively, these events cast an even darker cloud over Senator Benton's assertion that the road to Mexico would bring progress and prosperity to Indian people along the way.

Most of the alcohol consumed by the Kansas came from western Missouri by way of the overland road out of Westport. That road also served as an alcohol supply route for the Shawnees, whose reservation lay between the western Missouri distilleries and one at Council Grove, and for the Sacs and Foxes southwest of the Shawnees and the Miamis.[27] In 1843 Indian Office authorities in Washington were told that Mexican alcohol was being taken into present eastern Kansas, particularly to the Shawnees and the Sacs and Foxes, and that the amount was increasing dramatically.[28] The "petty" traders involved were mostly former employees of "legitimate companies" with no trade licenses and thus answered to no one but themselves.[29] Four years later, Upper Arkansas Agent Thomas Fitzpatrick reported to the Indian commissioner in Washington from Bent's Fort that most of these "murderous fellows" were from either Canada, Mexico, or Europe. He further reported that the Cheyennes and Arapahoes were increasing raids on the overland trains for alcohol; his efforts to counsel the Indians on the "deleterious effects" of alcohol had come to no avail.[30]

In 1835, it will be recalled,[31] an entire village camped near Bent's Fort was reportedly drunk. Two years later a crowded lodge of Dog Soldiers "went on a drinking spree" that culminated in Porcupine's drunken assault on Little Creek—and a major political schism in Cheyenne tribal affairs. Another account of the same incident has it that the entire encampment "was reduced to drunken chaos."[32] A more detailed account of Cheyenne drinking is that of Ohioan

Lewis Hector Garrard, who camped at Bent's Fort for several months in 1846 while awaiting a commercial transaction with some overland traders. At a point near the mouth of the Purgatoire, wrote Garrard, the doleful activities ensued:

> By five o'clock, we [the party from Bent's] were at the lower end of Tharp's bottom, where was corralling a United States train. . . . By ten o'clock, the baying of the Cheyenne village dogs was distinctly heard across the [Arkansas] river. After an hour's wandering in the tangled bottoms, Vipponah [a Cheyenne] welcomed us. The village was in an uproar. The "opposition traders" a mile above had conferred a present of liquor on several chiefs, who, in turn, disposed some of it to their friends, and all were making "the night hideous," in honor of the "rosy god"; for they have songs adapted to their orgies, more noisy and fierce than which were known to exist. . . . They fell weeping, in drunken seriousness, and the next moment peals of laughter issued from their mouths, whence but an instant before the blubbering accents of grief had proceeded. . . . We began [on the following morning] to trade briskly in robes—owing to the cold weather, plenty of buffalo, and liquor, which seemed to open the Indian's heart . . . before concluding a bargain.[33]

By contrast, in the area east of Council Grove among the Kansas, Osages, and emigrant Indians from the East, trade alcohol was acquired with money authorized as annuities by the various land-cession treaties. Shawnee income under treaties dating back to 1817, for example, totaled $829,000; for the Kansas and Osages under the treaties of 1825 alone, it was $160,000; and for the

"Don Fernando de Taos New Mexico," original engraving by W. W. H. Davis, 1857. Courtesy of Palace of Governors Photo Archives (NMHM/DCA), negative #071388.

Miamis, just south of the Shawnees within a few miles of the road to New Mexico, it was $885,000.[34] Annuities were not awarded to the Cheyennes and Arapahoes until the Fort Laramie Treaty of 1851, which provided $50,000 per annum to be shared with the Crow, Assinaboine, Gros Ventre, Mandan, Arikara, and Lakota Sioux nations.[35] In the meantime, animal skins, robes, and related products were the mainstay trade items for Indians on the upper Arkansas. Amounting to tens of thousands of dollars in value by the end of the Mexican-American War in 1848, these transactions were dominated by Bent, St. Vrain & Co., operating out of its trade center near the mouth of the Purgatoire. While the company was diligent in securing the requisite federal licenses to trade with certain Indians at certain places in Indian Country, it nevertheless used alcohol in a manner that, by the very act itself, violated the

Indian alcohol law of 1822, which required that a licensed trader's bonds be placed in suit if the licensee had any "ardent spirits" in his possession in Indian Country.[36]

This did not happen, raising the question as to how Bent, St. Vrain & Co. was able to avoid legal action year after year while supplying Indians of the upper Arkansas with alcohol for well over a decade. Even at New Bent's Fort, established in 1853 a few miles east after the original facility was abandoned by William Bent in 1849, the alcohol trade continued. In 1857 Upper Arkansas Indian Agent Robert C. Miller reported to officials in Washington that a large number of "small trade" Mexicans in the employ of William Bent were "going in and out" of the fort whenever they choose, "to trade their miserable Mexican whiskey" with the Indians.[37] All this occurred despite William Bent's own admonition two decades earlier regarding the "insidious power" of alcohol on Indians,[38] as well as a government report in 1847 that the Bents had ceased using alcohol in the Indian trade. "This laudable change in their business has not emanated from a regard for law," wrote Upper Arkansas Agent Thomas Fitzpatrick,

> nor from any philanthropic motives, but from the fact of it becoming a great nuisance, and very dangerous to those having large investments in the trade, and whose expenses were heavy; and not being able to compete successfully with numerous small traders who infest this country, and whose expenses are comparatively nothing—whose whole stock in trade amounted to only a few trinkets and three or four hundred gallons of liquor procured on the Missouri frontier, Mexico, or the Hudson Bay.[39]

In the meantime, one tactic for evading the law was to farm out the actual transactions to a secondary (and unlicensed) party. Such was the case in 1844 when William Tharp—well known for trading whiskey for robes at a Southern Cheyenne village near Big Timbers—consigned his robes to a nearby double log cabin built and operated by William Bent as a satellite to his main trading center west of the Purgatoire. It was a considerable operation, for less than a year later it was reported that Tharp and others, "coming down by way of Bent's Fort, and the Santa Fe trail," reached Westport with nearly 200 packs of furs and robes. The following spring, Tharp and his partners were on their way back to the upper Arkansas with seven wagonloads of "merchandise" that in all likelihood included alcohol for their operations at Big Timbers.[40]

A more favored stratagem of Bent, St. Vrain & Co. and other so-called regular traders for circumventing federal Indian prohibition laws was described by George Bird Grinnell, primarily based on interviews with George Bent (1843–1918), the mixed-blood son of William Bent and Owl Woman. Despite his assertion that "whites never get it right," George Bent was a respected Cheyenne historian and informant sought out by historians and other scholars throughout the land.[41]

According to Grinnell, a large quantity of liquor would be sent out by traders to a tribal village after repeated visits to the traders' camp by village chiefs had indicated the amount of liquor desired and how Indians would make payment. The traders would then arrive at the village and place kegs of alcohol of various sizes in the lodge of the chief. The Indians would go into the lodge and offer what they had to trade. Each Indian was then assigned a certain keg according to the number of robes (or horses) he wished to trade. He then tied a piece of colored string to the keg to mark it as his, but the keg remained sealed for the present. When all the trading was completed the trader left, and it was not until he was some distance from the village that the chief allowed individual Indians to take possession of their marked kegs and open them. On occasion, when Mexican traders would enter the village with more "ordinary" goods, some would slip kegs of alcohol to Indians for a higher price before regular traders learned of their presence. The result was widespread intoxication and an end to all so-called legitimate business until the kegs were empty and the Indians were sober once again.[42]

There was, according to Grinnell, a certain degree of moral legitimacy on the part of regular traders, as opposed to the Taos and Santa Fe traders who were the real culprits in debauching the Cheyennes and cheating them of their robes. Even so, such selective reckoning could not disguise the obvious fact that, however indirectly the regular traders operated, they too were trading alcohol for the products of the Indians' labor.

On another front, the alcohol trade with the Kiowas and Comanches along the overland roads rose perceptibly following the peace of 1840. After abandoning Old Bent's Fort in 1849, the Bents constructed their new facility near Big Timbers to the east. Not long thereafter it was reported from Council Grove that a large westbound wagon train owned by William Bent "was on its way to trade with the Comanches,"[43] who by that time, often in company with the Kiowas, were hunting and trading along the Arkansas from Great Bend west to the present Kansas-Colorado boundary.

In 1852, at newly established Fort Atkinson a few miles west of present Dodge City, Julius Froebel recorded that travelers could obtain all sorts of supplies and delicacies, including preserved oys-

"Arrival of the Caravan at Santa Fe," lithograph in Josiah Gregg, Commerce of the Prairies *(1844), courtesy of Kansas State Historical Society.*

ters, champagne, and other ardent spirits. Froebel also told of a Kiowa party that visited their camp near the fort.[44] Clearly, the overland road was a powerful attraction to Indians, and by the early 1860s it was widely known that "evil-disposed white men" were carrying on a brisk trade in alcohol with the Kiowas and Comanches. The only way to stop them, insisted military officials on the scene, was to have well-armed and mounted detachments patrol the road on a regular basis between the Little Arkansas and Walnut Creek.[45]

But as expected, this was summarily rejected by the War Department on fiscal grounds. In the meantime, in a "peace, friendship, and amity" treaty convened at Fort Atkinson in 1853, the Kiowas and Comanches were awarded $18,000 in annuities for ten years, to be paid in merchandise "or in a shape best adapted to their wants," thereby providing them with an additional and certainly more businesslike means of acquiring alcohol.[46]

By the mid-1850s the Walnut Creek crossing near Great Bend emerged as a major alcohol market for the Kiowas and Comanches. Here, in the summer of 1855, William Allison and Francis Booth established a "ranch" for the purpose of "setting up trade with the Kiowas and Comanches." Within a year Allison was reported to have shipped 10,000 pounds of dried bison tongues east from his Great Bend facility while providing "poor whiskey" to overland travelers and the Indians. Following Allison's death in 1859, George Peacock—who had clerked for William Bent and learned the details of how the Indian alcohol trade actually worked—took over the Allison operation. By then it included a mail station, general store, well-stocked tavern, haying operation, and alcohol outlet for Indians, some of whom played an important role in Peacock's violent death in 1860, apparently the result of an alcohol transaction gone sour. Peacock's successor at Walnut Creek was Charles Rath, who three years later successfully defied a military order obtained by the Indian Office to shut down his alcohol business with the Plains tribes, on grounds that his operations were not legally in Indian Country and therefore not in violation of federal law.[47]

In the meantime, overland travelers were pleased to learn of new facilities and services on the road west. In 1858, a newspaper with the masthead "KANSAS CITY," informed non-Indian travelers regarding the amenities available to those who were heading to the

Colorado mines or, perhaps, to Taos or Santa Fe. The word "entertainment" as listed in the "KANSAS CITY" newspaper was in fact code for alcohol in its various forms—alcohol that could be purchased in what was still federally administered and regulated Indian Country:

> "Jack Point [42 miles west of Westport]: Wood, water, grass, *entertainment*"
>
> "Palmyra [56 miles west of Westport]: Mail station, wood, water, grass and *entertainment*"
>
> "110 Mile Creek [73 miles west of Westport]: Mail station, coal, wood, grass, *entertainment*"
>
> "142 Creek [101 miles west of Westport]: *Entertainment*, wood, water, grass"
>
> "Council Grove [121 miles west of Westport]: Mail station, wood, water, and *groceries*"
>
> "Diamond Spring [137 miles west of Westport]: Mail station, *entertainment*, wood, water, grass, corn"
>
> "Cottonwood (river) [167 1/2 miles west of Westport]: Mail station, *entertainment*, corn, hay, wood, water, grass, provisions"
>
> "Allison's Ranch [253 miles west of Westport]: Corn, hay, *tavern*, provisions, Indians, Buffalo"
>
> "Bent's Fort [520 miles west of Westport]: *Everything necessary* for men and animals"[48]

It is worth remembering that such trappings of the white man's civilization were also open to Indians with trade goods or annuity dollars to spend. Decades earlier, Senator Benton had firmly proclaimed that Indian settlements along the overland highway would lead to tribal improvement and contribute to "the preservation and improvement of their own race."[49] By the late 1850s, however, Benton had turned his attention to railroads, a technologically superior mode of transportation that soon would replace pack mules and the cumbersome Murphy wagons. This would open up the prairie-plains to a multitude of white men with land grants and the plow—not to more Indians.

The discovery of gold along the Front Range of the Colorado Rockies in 1858 was followed by mounting difficulties between Plains tribes and invading whites, which led to the irresolute Fort Wise Treaty of 1861, the Sand Creek Massacre of 1864, the Little Arkansas Treaties of 1865, and the Medicine Lodge Treaties of 1867 that finally forced the Southern Cheyennes, Arapahoes, Kiowas, and Comanches to accept the reality of concentrated reservation life in future Oklahoma. As well, the rapid reduction of the central and southern bison herds only hastened their move to reservation life. By 1871 the Kansas and Osages, and most of the emigrant tribes west of Missouri, had also been forced to take up residence in future Oklahoma. Most adult members of these tribes were by then well acquainted with the mystifying powers of alcohol, and some were consuming the potentially deadly product in excess.

In 1866 an important but little publicized federal law authorized important changes in Indian alcohol law dating back to the 1820s. Introduced by Senator James W. Grimes of Iowa and urged forward by most western businessmen, it led to bickering between the Departments of Interior and War over administrative control of Indian policy, and eventually a law providing that "any moral and lawful citizen" who, after posting bond and obtaining a permit from a district judge or U.S. attorney, might freely engage in the Indian trade.[50] Federal Indian liquor laws, of course, remained in effect.

But no longer could Indian Office officials deter entrepreneurs from dealing with Indians simply by not granting them licenses. Local attorneys and judges anxious to promote the economic interests of their constituents welcomed the opportunity to even scores with federal Indian agents and superintendents who had failed to cooperate in the past.

10

Roads Unregulated

Responding to pressure from the overland trading community, the federal government provided military protection along the so-called national road west of Missouri, up to the international boundary, first in 1829, 1833, and 1834, on two occasions in 1843, and again in 1845.[1] During the Mexican-American War (1846–1848), Fort Mann was constructed on the northern bank of the Arkansas about 8 miles west of present Dodge City. Added to this list prior to the Civil War were Fort Atkinson in 1850, a few miles west of Fort Mann (which was abandoned in 1850); Fort Union in 1851, on the mountain branch of the Santa Fe road some 25 miles northeast of present Las Vegas, New Mexico; and Fort Larned (first called Camp on Pawnee Fork) in 1859, on the right bank of the Pawnee River 8 miles above its confluence with the Arkansas. During the Civil War the following installations were established: Fort Lyon in 1861, near present Lamar, Colorado; Fort Zarah in 1864, near the mouth of Walnut Creek and the Great Bend of the Arkansas; Fort

Aubry in 1865, a few miles north of the Arkansas River near the Kansas-Colorado border; and Fort Dodge in 1865, on the left bank of the Arkansas a few miles east of present Dodge City.[2]

This dizzying array of facilities, designed to ward off enemy attacks, was not strictly composed of defensive fortifications. Rather, they were mainly designed to provide dwellings for troops and storage for supplies in remote areas of actual or anticipated violence against American interests.[3] They also were centers for organizing military campaigns against hostile (or supposedly hostile) Indians, and they became embarkation points for protecting overland commerce and mail. On balance it appears that mail escorts, as requested by the Post Office and/or private mail contractors, were adequately funded and mostly successful. By 1861 the safety of overland commerce was much improved over what it had been in the immediate years after the Mexican-American War. Even so, according to a balanced study of the matter, this would soon change, for the Civil War era witnessed Indian hostilities more severe than those encountered in any previous period in the history of the overland roads.[4] Clearly, the Sand Creek Massacre in November 1864, as well as General Winfield Hancock's disastrous expedition west of Fort Larned three years later—both less than a day's travel from the Santa Fe road—did little to lessen worry and resentment among Indians and white traders in western Kansas and eastern Colorado Territory.

Yet Section 2 of the Trade and Intercourse Act of March 2, 1847, provided prison sentences of up to two years for anyone convicted in a district court of the United States of "selling, exchanging, bartering, giving, disposing, introducing, or even attempting to introduce" alcohol in any form to an Indian in Indian Country.[5] Not surprisingly, the 1847 law created a furor among alcohol traders along the overland roads to New Mexico, as well as among eastern lobbyists seeking to overthrow the law, or at least see it sparingly enforced. Surely it is to Indian Commissioner William Medill's lasting credit that he refused to be swayed by the lobbyists and Benton's people by summarily dismissing their cynical and harmful proposals "with ill-disguised hostility."[6]

Enforcement was the overriding problem, as became apparent during the war with Mexico. In 1847, newspapers in St. Louis and New York reported renewed Indian attacks on military supply lines, mainly along the roads to Taos and Santa Fe, thereby placing other U.S. military efforts in jeopardy. In response, the War Department authorized the enlistment of three volunteer infantry companies, composed of recent Dutch and German emigrants to Missouri, mainly because other Missourians simply refused to do even garrison duty in Indian Country. Between the fall of 1847 and the late summer of 1848, the so-called Indian Battalion commanded by Lieutenant Colonel William Gilpin conducted a series of maneuvers from Fort Mann against "Indians of the upper Arkansas." The action was successful enough to allow Indian Office officials to report, in October 1848, that fewer robberies had taken place on the overland road than during the previous two years.[7]

But there were problems nevertheless—serious problems related to alcohol. Toward the end of May 1848, after Commander Gilpin had confiscated and destroyed sixty gallons of beer brought to Fort Mann by a German trader from the Fort Riley area, some of his enlisted men vented their wrath by destroying all of the so-called hospital wine and brandy then being transported by a seventy-five-wagon caravan supposedly headed for Chihuahua.[8] The following winter, Fort Mann commander Captain William Pelzer was reportedly intoxicated on a "regular" basis, while some of his subordinates entertained themselves with heavy drinking and shooting at one

Current view of Bent's Old Fort, National Historic Site, reconstructed in 1976. Author's photograph.

another while on "hunting expeditions" that, on one occasion, led to an accidental fatality.[9]

An officer of the New York Volunteers returning east in 1848 described Fort Mann as "a little government post, or half-way depot, garrisoned by a handful of volunteers, who drank corn whiskey . . . and otherwise wore out their lives in the service of their country."[10] The situation at Fort Mann was not unique. Indian Agent I. C. Taylor at Fort Zarah in the mid-1860s was "constantly drunk" and sold whiskey to Indians from his official quarters at the Fort; at nearby Fort Larned a post commander was discharged for habitual drunkenness; and less than a year prior to the Sand Creek Massacre the Indian Office in Washington was informed that if Indians were allowed to visit military posts without escorts it was impossible to prevent their young men from getting whiskey or their women from being demoralized. And at Fort Dodge in 1868, the men of a military detachment sent to intercept and hopefully confiscate a whiskey shipment from northern Mexico headed for Indian Country were so drunk that several of them died before their failed expedition had returned to its post on the Arkansas.[11]

There was little enforcement of the Indian alcohol laws or apprehension of suspected violators. In fact, veteran alcohol traders were surprised to encounter so little surveillance and policing of their activities. A case in point was an incident at Fort Mann in February 1848 when Upper Arkansas Indian Agent Thomas Fitzpatrick called on Colonel Gilpin and a company of his Indian Battalion to pursue "a whiskey party from Taos" heading toward an undesignated point in Indian Country. Gilpin refused because of disputes with Agent Fitzpatrick over the administration of Indian affairs in general and the enforcement of the Indian Trade and Intercourse laws in particular.[12]

Indian Agent Richard Cummins intervened in support of Fitzpatrick by suggesting to Indian Office authorities in St. Louis that more "positive orders" should have been issued to Colonel Gilpin, as well as to other military detachments operating on or near the overland road. That, of course, did not happen, and during the remainder of the year more than 10,000 persons freely traveled the road between Missouri and Taos or Santa Fe. Only one trader's illegal dealings in Indian Country were called into question: an unsuspecting German trader whose sixty gallons of beer were dumped on the ground by Colonel Gilpin at Fort Mann.[13] Whether this trader had any understanding whatsoever regarding how illegal alcohol was actually marketed in Indian Country is doubtful; more certain is that he was neither arrested nor brought to trial.[14]

Cummins also sought to have the commander at Fort Leavenworth intervene in the Gilpin matter, but to no avail.[15] From his headquarters near the Santa Fe road a few miles west of the Missouri line, the Indian agent had dispatched a letter to Indian Superintendent William Harvey in which he presented a detailed analysis of the problem and what he considered an effective means of halting the conveyance of alcohol to Indians in Indian Country. Prefacing his remarks was the statement that most Indian agents were afraid to solicit help from the military because they would be turned down "and worsted in the end." Such unacceptable conduct, continued Cummins, should be publicized in the St. Louis and Independence newspapers as a means of correcting "wrong impressions" about actual events in the vast country west of Missouri. Specifically, Cummins requested that the commissioner of Indian affairs in Washington make arrangements for a troop of at least thirty mounted men under the command of "an active and prudent officer" to "regularly patrol" the road from Westport to Council Grove, and perhaps as far west as Bent's Fort on the Arkansas, with instructions to search all wagons leaving from or heading toward the western border of Missouri.[16]

But Cummins's recommendations fell on deaf ears, and the flow of alcohol into Indian Country continued. In fact, it may have increased, given the conversation that ensued between the Fort Leavenworth Agency and the St. Louis Superintendency in 1847. When Cummins reported that many Indian alcohol traders were "under a wrong impression"[17] regarding what they assumed were lawful activities on their part, he redirected the conversation back to the Kansa and Osage treaties of 1825, whereby Senator Benton and his aides had asserted that the overland roads *through* Indian Country were public highways and thus *not legally a part of Indian Country.*

Some of the traders, however, were less certain. Agent Fitzpatrick reported in September 1847 that the Bents had ceased selling liquor directly to the Indians, "finding it more unprofitable than obeying the law."[18] Others, mainly smaller traders, remained confident that the 1847 law did not apply to them so long as they stayed on Benton's road. To this Agent Cummins responded that most of the traders claimed to be true Santa Fe traders "only until they got out of reach of the authorities," at which point they would leave the road to trade with whomever they wished—including Indians. No response came from his superiors in St. Louis and Washington, and early the next year he reported that the bulk of the overland trade for the coming season was intended to be in alcohol. Even the sutler for troops stationed near the Arkansas crossing of the Santa Fe road, said Cummins, was stocking a large supply of spirituous liquors, much of it, presumably, in anticipation of the forthcoming alcohol trade season.[19]

It was indeed a banner year for traders, including some Indians who ventured into dealings on their own. In 1847 the Osages, who had more experience with alcohol than the Comanches,[20] traded two years of annuity payments ($24,000) to the Comanches for 1,500 mules valued at no less that $60,000. On their Neosho River reservation southeast of Council Grove, the Osages traded 500 of the mules for as many gallons of whiskey, amounting to $40 per gallon. "The ensuing drunken revelries," reported the Osage agent, "made the entire region unsafe for whites and Indians alike." Joining the Osages as traders were the Kansas, who in 1850 were described as "great whiskey dealers as well as drinkers," wrote one government official. "They often travel a distance of two or three hundred miles for whiskey, making it convenient to steal . . . as they pass along, and exchange in the same with the miserable whites along the [Santa Fe] line for whiskey."[21]

In 1853 Agent Fitzpatrick reported from his upper Arkansas post that the trade and intercourse laws designed to protect Indians from alcohol were in fact "nothing but a dead letter." The great number of white emigrants constantly passing through that section of the country, he reported later, "pay no regard to such restrictions; they traffic without license, furnish liquor to the Indians, and render all efforts to regulate the intercourse laws a mere farce."[22]

A year later Kansas Territory was officially organized; its first legislative session declared the Santa Fe road an official "territorial road" from the Missouri line to Council Grove.[23] In the same session, convened at the Shawnee Methodist Mission near the overland road, "An Act to restrain dram shops and taverns, and to regulate the sale of intoxicating liquor" was passed, which authorized a penalty for selling alcohol to Indians without a territorial license. As with previous federal statutes on the same matter, there is little evidence that the new law was enforced with any dedication, if at all.[24] That same year Allison and Booth established their "ranch" at Walnut Crossing, primarily to trade with Kiowas and Comanches; by 1862 it was reported by a military official that "evil-disposed white men" at Walnut Crossing were promoting a brisk whiskey trade with local tribes—in fact it was the very reason they were there.[25] Alcohol, it seemed, was everywhere.

In a response to the discovery of gold in 1858 northwest of present Denver and a veritable multitude of would-be argonauts heading across the Plains for such mining centers as Central City,

Blackhawk, and Gold Hill, a Colorado paper reported that eighty wagons with a consignment of 1,600 barrels of alcohol and 2,700 cases of champagne were heading for the area.[26] The announcement was posted on November 30, 1864, a day after the Sand Creek Massacre in which scores of Southern Cheyennes and Arapahoes were killed by Colonel John M. Chivington and his volunteer troops on a tributary of the upper Arkansas north of present Lamar, Colorado. Whether alcohol was directly or indirectly involved in this atrocity is unclear; undeniable is that by the mid-1860s alcohol had become a staple for both sides in the unfolding cultural confrontation on the plains of eastern Colorado and western Kansas. The overland road opened by William Becknell in 1821, expanded along other routes in ensuing decades, played a conspicuous role in fueling that confrontation. And throughout this period, the question of *whose* roads they actually were remained in doubt, as much as *what* the vast place called Indian Country actually was—politically, economically, and legally.

But legally, the problem simply would not go away. In the late spring of 1866, from his temporary headquarters at Fort Zarah near Walnut Crossing, Kiowa-Comanche Agent Jesse H. Leavenworth demanded clarity regarding the legal boundaries of Indian Country. It was a serious matter, he informed Indian Commissioner Dennis Cooley in Washington; a renegade whiskey trader named Dietz operating on what he claimed was his own land near Fort Zarah had threatened Leavenworth with legal action if he were expelled from Indian Country for having provided the Kiowas and Comanches "with all the alcohol they wanted."[27] No response was recorded (or preserved) in the Indian Office or War Department files. Perhaps this was because the recent tragedy at Sand Creek, followed by the controversial Little Arkansas Treaties in 1865, the loosening of trade licenses in 1866,[28] and the Hancock debacle west of Fort Larned a year later, damaged Indian-white relations so greatly that the decision of least resistance was simply to ignore Leavenworth's demands.

This brings us back to Senator Benton and the national road issue in Indian Country. The notion that simply marking and surveying an overland road through Indian Country caused it to be a public highway (and therefore not subject to the laws of Indian Country, as many traders insisted) was belief, not fact. In fact, the 1834 law was unambiguous in its description of Indian Country boundaries; indeed, its very clarity distinguished it from all previous legislation. By 1834 as well, the Supreme Court had confirmed the federal government's plenary authority over Indian peoples. In the meantime, treaty after treaty approved by the Senate forced Indian nations to cede or take possession of specifically described acreage in Indian Country, often through separate articles within the same treaty.

Rights-of-way across such parcels in no way altered the area covered in Indian Country as set forth in 1834 and subsequently clarified by the Supreme Court in 1877, when it ruled that Indian Country remained such so long as Indians retained title to the land; it ceased being Indian Country whenever and wherever they lost title, absent any conflicting proviso by any treaty or act of Congress.[29] Because the $500 (in cash and merchandise) given to the Osages and Kansas under the right-of-way treaties of 1825 were for "privileges granted," not payment for land, the two tribes lost title to none of their lands by those treaties.[30] Given the ease with which many, perhaps most, alcohol traders evaded the Indian alcohol laws in Indian Country,[31] it is tempting to conclude that arguing the pros and cons regarding whether the roads to Taos and Santa Fe were legally a part of Indian Country may be less important than trying to understand why enforcement of the Indian prohibition laws in Indian Country was so difficult and, in certain cases, impossible.[32]

There are several plausible explanations: the long distances and remoteness of Indian Country in 1834; austerity in federal military expenditures, prompting reduction of the regular army from 10,000 to 6,000 men in 1821, the same year William Becknell opened the route to New Mexico; lack of military support for undermanned Indian agents in the field; an ineffective and often anti-Indian frontier court system;[33] and, of course, the bureaucratic snarls in the administration of federal Indian policy, including the activities of "Indian Rings" (allegedly composed of corrupt federal officials and businessmen allied in defrauding Indians and directing an otherwise philanthropic Indian policy to their own selfish ends).[34] Each of these has some merit for understanding what may have caused the Indian trade to become so deadly. But financial austerity and lack of military support for apprehending, or at least trying to apprehend, outlaw traders roaming the overland roads rank near the top.

During the time of dramatic fiscal austerity prior to the Mexican-American War, Congress funded a half-dozen military escorts, mainly to the benefit of overland merchants and traders. Between 1847 and 1865 it authorized the construction and garrisoning of nine military posts on or near the roads to Taos and Santa Fe. In 1851 it funded a special military patrol designed to engender a sense of power and fear among Indians along the road between Fort Atkinson and Fort Union. And from 1853 to 1858 it paid for federal mail escorts when needed, as determined by the War Department or officials of the private mail contractors.[35] And, of course, the war with Mexico did not bankrupt the nation's treasury. In short, public money was made available for protecting merchants, traders, western travelers, and a two-year war—but not for protecting a few thousand Indians from odious alcohol traders in Indian Country.

Senator Benton, who in the 1850s turned his attention to transcontinental railroads and the opening of Indian Country to greater white settlement, did not promote the survey and marking of a national road to create an artery of transportation legally separate from the vast Indian domain. That was the task and goal of traders and their associates. What Benton (and those he represented) did was establish and then promote a setting and political strategy for rumor and misinformation to be accepted as reality. In the ensuing trade, thousands of Plains and emigrant Indians along the roads from Missouri to New Mexico were encouraged to embrace alcohol and/or annuity dollars as acceptable and even preferred payment for processed bison robes and other bison products. All things considered, it was—as the white traders sought to justify their business model—a lucrative endeavor in the best interests of themselves *and* their less sophisticated Indian clients.

Such was not the case. Beyond the appalling deception and misery experienced by most Indians seeking a better life from trade, the alcohol trade was no less abhorrent under the federal alcohol laws for Indian Country. Fleshed out in detail after much debate in Congress during the two and a half decades following William Becknell's first journey to New Mexico, enforcement was often ignored by the federal government at virtually all levels. Insufficient funding, bureaucratic snarls following the transfer of Indian policy administration to civilian control in 1849, and, more often than not, heavy-handed opportunism and corruption at a personal level only made matters worse. The result was a dramatic decline of the

Indian population in the area traversed by the overland roads from western Missouri to northern New Mexico. This provided a template for more deadly dealings in other places where Indians resided or would be forced to reside by the Great Father in Washington.

Notes

Introduction

1. Private Council with the Delaware and Shawnee Chiefs, n.d., 1834, Letters Received by the Office of Indian Affairs, St. Louis Superintendency, RG75, M234, R752, National Archives and Records Administration.

2. William Bent correspondence, passim, April 27, 1859–October 17, 1860, Letters Received by the Office of Indian Affairs, Upper Arkansas Agency, RG75, M234, R878, National Archives and Records Administration.

3. David D. Mitchell to T. Hartley Crawford, October 25, 1841, Letters Received by the Office of Indian Affairs, St. Louis Superintendency, RG75, M234, R752, National Archives and Records Administration; Mitchell to Crawford, September 12, 1842, *Annual Report of the Commissioner of Indian Affairs* (1842), NCR 872, R4158, 425–426.

Chapter 1. Before Becknell

1. See, for example, Ray Allen Billington, *Westward Expansion: A History of the American Frontier* (New York: Macmillan Company, 3rd ed., 1967), 463; LeRoy R. Hafen, W. Eugene Hollon, and Carl Coke Rister, *Western America* (Englewood Cliffs, NJ: Prentice-Hall, Inc., 3rd ed., 1970), 187; Kent Ladd Steckmesser, *The Westward Movement: A Short History* (New York: McGraw-Hill, 1969), 208; Robert W. Richmond, *Kansas: A Land of Contrasts* (Arlington Heights, IL: Forum Press, 3rd ed., 1989), 45; Larry Beachum, *William*

Becknell, Father of the Santa Fe Trail (El Paso: Texas Western Press, 1982), title page.

2. Robert Glass Cleland, *This Reckless Breed of Men: The Trappers and Fur Traders of the Southwest* (New York: Alfred A. Knopf, 1963), 129.

3. For a convenient summary of the question as to whether Becknell actually planned to travel to Santa Fe, including the views of Josiah Gregg, Max Morehead, Marc Simons, Larry Beachum, and David Weber, see Michael L. Olson and Harry C. Meyers, "The Diary of Pedro Ignacio Gallego Wherein 400 Soldiers Following the Trail of the Comanches Met William Becknell on His First Trip to Santa Fe," *Best of Wagon Tracks* 7, no. 1 (November 1992), n.p., http://www.santafetrail.org/wagontracks/DIARY_OF_PEDRO_IGNACIO_GALLEGO.pdf (accessed January 14, 2010).

4. John Francis Bannon, *The Spanish Borderlands Frontier, 1513–1821* (New York: Holt, Rinehart and Winston, 1970), 141; Donald J. Blakeslee, *Along Ancient Trails: The Mallet Expedition of 1739* (Niwot: University Press of Colorado, 1995), 55–64.

5. Bannon, *The Spanish Borderlands Frontier*, 141–142; Blakeslee, *Along Ancient Trails*, 182–183.

6. Blakeslee, *Along Ancient Trails*, 195–196; Bannon, *The Spanish Borderlands Frontier*, 142; Richard Edward Oglesby, *Manuel Lisa and the Opening of the Missouri Fur Trade* (Norman: University of Oklahoma Press, 1963), 35–37, 146.

7. William H. Goetzmann, *Exploration and Empire: The Explorer and Scientist in the Winning of the American West* (New York: Alfred A. Knopf, 1966), 14.

8. Bannon, *The Spanish Borderlands Frontier*, 215; Louise Barry, *The Beginning of the West: Annals of the Kansas Gateway to the American West, 1540–1854* (Topeka: Kansas State Historical Society, 1972), 68–69, 76–77; Leo E. Oliva, *Soldiers on the Santa Fe Trail* (Norman: University of Oklahoma Press, 1967), 6–7.

9. Frederic J. Athearn, *A Forgotten Empire: The Spanish Frontier in Colorado and New Mexico, 1540–1821* (Denver: Bureau of Land Management, Colorado Office, 1989), 73; Blakeslee, *Along Ancient Trails*, 44; Pekka Hämäläinen, "The Western Comanche Trade Center: Rethinking the Plains Indian Trade System," *Western Historical Quarterly* 29, no. 4 (Winter 1998): 506.

10. See J. Evatts Haley, "The Comanchero Trade," *Southwestern Historical Quarterly* 38, no. 3 (January 1935): 157–176, for a summary of this trade that began as a result of an understanding between New Mexico governor Juan Baptista de Anza and the Comanches in 1786.

11. A judicious treatment of Pike's controversial expedition to the upper

Arkansas and New Mexico in 1806–1807 is in Goetzmann, *Exploration and Empire*, 49–53.

12. Stephen G. Hyslop, *Bound for Santa Fe: The Road to New Mexico and the American Conquest, 1806–1848* (Norman: University of Oklahoma Press, 2002), 40–41; Barry, *The Beginning of the West*, 97; Olsen and Meyers, "The Diary of Pedro Ignacio Gallego."

13. Charles I. Bevans, ed., "Adams-Onis Treaty of 1819," *Treaties and Other International Agreements of the United States of America, 1776–1949* (Wallace L McKeehan, 1997–2001), 2, http://www.tamu.edu/ccbn/dewitt/adamonis.htm (accessed July 7, 2010).

14. Elbert B. Smith, *Magnificent Missourian: Thomas Hart Benton* (Philadelphia: Lippencott, 1957). Also see William Nisbet Chambers, *Old Bullion Benton, Senator from the New West: Thomas Hart Benton, 1782–1858* (Boston: Little, Brown and Company, 1956).

15. Herman J. Viola, *Thomas L. McKenney, Architect of America's Early Indian Policy: 1816–1830* (Chicago: Swallow Press, 1974), 65–69.

Chapter 2. "Vacant" Land

1. Goetzmann, *Exploration and Empire*, 62, 64; Horace Greeley, *An Overland Journey from New York to San Francisco in the Summer of 1859* (New York: C. M. Saxton, Barker & Co., 1860), 128 ff.

2. Homer E. Socolofsky and Huber Self, *Historical Atlas of Kansas* (Norman: University of Oklahoma Press, 1972), 4.

3. August Storrs to Senator Thomas Hart Benton, January 17, 1825, under the title of "Collocation of Indians," *Niles' Weekly Register*, February 24, 1825. Also see William E. Unrau, *The Rise and Fall of Indian Country, 1825–1855* (Lawrence: University Press of Kansas, 2007), 30–32.

4. There was no potable water available on the 60-mile stretch called *La Jornada* ("The Journey"), between the Middle Crossing of the Arkansas and the Lower Cimarron Spring.

5. Albert Pike, *Prose Sketches and Poems Written in the Western Country (with Additional Stories)*, rpt. ed., ed. David J. Weber (College Station: Texas A&M University Press, 1987), 282, cited in Hyslop, *Bound for Santa Fe*, 182.

6. Ibid.

7. Richard White, *"It's Your Misfortune and None of My Own": A History of the American West* (Norman: University of Oklahoma Press, 1991), 216.

8. In the 1840s, for example, tens of thousands of bison in Comancheria (the Comanche domain south of the Arkansas River to the Pecos and Colorado Valleys in southern Texas) were harvested by people not living there, including the Cheyennes and Arapahoes. See Pekka Hämäläinen, *The Comanche Empire* (New Haven: Yale University Press, 2008), 295.

9. Barry, *The Beginning of the West*, 201–203; Wayne Gard, *The Buffalo Hunters* (New York: Alfred A. Knopf, 1959), 57.

10. In 1807 President Jefferson appointed William Clark as brigadier general of the Louisiana Territorial Militia and United States Indian agent for the tribes of Louisiana Territory; Jerome O. Steffen, *William Clark: Jeffersonian Man on the Frontier* (Norman: University of Oklahoma Press), 1977), 53.

11. Thomas D. Isern, ed., "Exploration and Diplomacy: George Champlin Sibley's Report to William Clark," *Missouri Historical Review* 73, no. 1 (October 1978): 85–86.

12. George C. Sibley to David Barton, January 10, 1824, George C. Sibley Papers, Missouri Historical Society.

13. Jefferson to John Breckenridge, August 11, 1803; see Paul Leicester Ford, ed., *The Works of Thomas Jefferson* (New York: G. P. Putnam's Sons, 1905), vol. 10, 6–7.

14. Rev. Jedidiah Morse, *Report to the Secretary of War of the United States on Indian Affairs, Comprising a Narrative of a Tour Performed in the Summer of 1820* (New Haven, CT: S. Converse, 1822), 366–367, table.

15. Hämäläinen, *The Comanche Empire*, 347.

16. Elliott West, *The Contested Plains: Indians, Goldseekers, and the Rush to Colorado* (Lawrence: University Press of Kansas, 1998), 67.

17. Ibid., 64–73.

18. In 1831 Upper Missouri Indian Agent John Doughtery reported that in upper Missouri country "2,200 packs of buffalo robes [had] been purchased [from Indians] for whiskey at 24 to 34 dollars per gallon"; Dougherty to William Clark, November 10, 1831, Letters Received by the Office of Indian Affairs, St. Louis Superintendency, RG75, M234, R749, National Archives and Records Administration.

19. *U.S. Statutes at Large*, vol. 4: 411–412 (1830).

20. Ibid., 371; *Indian Land Cessions in the United States, Eighth Annual Report of the Bureau of American Ethnology* (1896–1897), pt. 2, comp. Charles C. Royce (Washington, DC: Government Printing Office, 1889), 793.

21. Roger L. Nichols, *General Henry Atkinson: A Western Military Career* (Norman: University of Oklahoma Press, 1965), 48–68. Fort Missouri was renamed Fort Atkinson on January 5, 1821, and abandoned on June 6, 1827, on

the recommendation of the U.S. Army inspector general, who held that the post "served no useful purpose, was unhealthful, and was too far from the starting point of the Santa Fe Trail." Robert W. Frazer, *Forts of the West: Military Forts and Presidios and Posts Commonly Called Forts West of the Mississippi River to 1898* (Norman: University of Oklahoma Press, 1965), 84–85.

22. Charles J. Kappler, comp., *Indian Affairs: Law and Treaties*, vol. 2, *Treaties* (Washington, DC: Government Printing Office, 1904), 225–246.

23. Ibid., 230–234, 244–246, 258–260; Nichols, *General Henry Atkinson*, 98.

24. Kappler, *Treaties*, 262–264.

25. Ibid., 370.

26. Josiah Gregg, *Commerce of the Prairies*, ed. Max L. Moorhead (Norman: University of Oklahoma Press, 1954), 332.

27. Walter A. Schroeder, "Spread of Settlement in Howard County, Missouri, 1810–1859," *Missouri Historical Review* 58, no. 2 (October 1968): 9–12; Floyd Calvin Shoemaker, *Missouri's Struggle for Statehood, 1804–1821* (Jefferson City, MO: Hugh Stephens Printing Co., 1916), 68–69.

28. Lewis E. Atherton, "James and Robert Aull—A Frontier Mercantile Firm," *Missouri Historical Review* 30, no. 1 (October 1935): 3–9.

29. Charles N. Glaab, "Business Patterns in the Growth of a Midwestern City: The Kansas City Business Community Before the Civil War," *Business History Review*, 33, no. 2 (Summer 1959): 167; William E. Unrau, *White Man's Wicked Water: The Alcohol Trade and Prohibition in Indian Country, 1802–1892* (Lawrence: University Press of Kansas, 1996), 31.

30. Taos County Historical Society, "The Taos Grist Mill of Ceran St. Vrain Believed Established in 1850," http://www/taos-history.org/unit/s-v-001.html, 1–4, 9 (accessed March 6, 2010).

Chapter 3. Cleared Land

1. Francis Paul Prucha, *American Indian Treaties: The History of a Political Anomaly* (Berkeley: University of California Press, 1994), 1.

2. Blakeslee, *Along Ancient Trails*, 30; William E. Unrau, "The Depopulation of the Dheghia-Siouan Kansa Prior to Removal," *New Mexico Historical Review* 48, no. 4 (October 1973): 316.

3. David I. Bushnell Jr., "Villages of the Algonquian, Siouan, and Caddoan Tribes West of the Mississippi," Bureau of American Ethnology *Bulletin* 83 (1927): 77; William E. Unrau, *The Kansa Indians: A History of the Wind People, 1673–1873* (Norman: University of Oklahoma Press, 1971), 6; William E.

Unrau, *Indians of Kansas: The Euro-American Conquest of Indian Kansas* (Topeka: Kansas State Historical Society, 1991), 31.

4. "A Map Exhibiting the Territorial Limits of several Indian Nations & Tribes of Indians agreeable to the notes of A. Chouteau reduced, & laid down on a scale of 80 miles to the inch," by R. Paul, February 1816, Map 884, Tube 702, Record Group 75, Cartographic Branch, National Archives and Records Administration.

5. Steffen, *William Clark*, 97–98; Unrau, *The Rise and Fall of Indian Country*, 82–83; Paul, "Map Exhibiting the Territorial Limits of several Nations & Tribes."

6. Prucha, *American Indian Treaties*, 126–128; Kappler, *Treaties*, 95–99.

7. Clarence E. Carter, ed., *The Territorial Papers of the United States*, vol. 14 (Washington, DC: Government Printing Office, 1950): 199, 242, 344.

8. Donald Jackson, "Journey to the Mandans, 1809: The Lost Narrative of Dr. Thomas," Missouri Historical Society *Bulletin* 10, no. 3 (April 1964): 184. Ezekiel Williams, one of Manual Lisa's hunters, reported in 1811 that the Kansas "rarely, if ever, have been known to spill blood of a white man [but] when a white hunter is found on their lands, they take his furs & his arms; he is then beaten with ramrods and driven off." "Ezekiel Williams' Adventures in Colorado," Missouri Historical Society *Collections* 4, no. 2 (1913): 199–205; and Frederic F. Voelker, "Ezekiel Williams of Boon's Lick," Missouri Historical Society *Bulletin* 8, no. 1 (October 1951): 218.

9. William E. Unrau, "George C. Sibley's Plea for the 'Garden of Missouri' in 1824," Missouri Historical Society *Bulletin* 17, no. 1 (October 1970): 6.

10. "Memorandum of a preliminary arrangement (for the purchase and sale of lands) made on the 20th day of September 1818 at Fort Osage between G. C. Sibley [?] of Ind affairs for the U. States acting in this matter under instructions from His Execy Governor Clark on the one part and the chiefs and head men of the Kansas nation on the other part," Sibley Papers.

11. George C. Sibley to William Clark, November 5, 1818, Indian Papers, Missouri Historical Society.

12. *U.S. Statutes at Large*, vol. 3: 141, 145 (1802).

13. Ibid., 15–16.

14. Sibley to Clark, February 3, 1819, Carter, *Territorial Papers*, 15: 516.

15. Cleland, *The Reckless Breed of Men*, 129–130.

16. Andrew C. Isenberg, "The Market Revolution in the Borderlands: George Champlin Sibley in Missouri and New Mexico, 1808–1826," *Journal of the Early Republic* 21, no. 3 (Autumn 2001): 459.

17. Sibley to David Barton, January 10, 1824, Sibley Papers.

18. "Proposition to Extinguish Indian Title to Lands in Missouri," Com-

municated to the Senate, May 14, 1824, *American State Papers, Indian Affairs*, vol. 2 (Washington, DC: Gales and Seaton, 1834): 512. Map of State of Kansas, Compiled chiefly from the official records of the General Land Office, with supplemental data from other mapmaking agencies, under the direction of L. P. Berthrong, Chief of Drafting Division, GLO, 1925, *Kansa or Kaw Indians vs. United States* (Court of Claims F-64) June 1, 1932, Map 11321, Tube 1387, RG75, Cartographic Branch, National Archives and Records Administration.

19. Kappler, *Treaties*, 217, 222.

20. Ibid., 247, 249; *The Road to Santa Fe: The Journal and Diaries of George Champlin Sibley Pertaining to the Surveying and Marking of a Road from the Missouri Frontier to the Settlements of New Mexico, 1825–1827*, ed. Kate L. Gregg (Albuquerque: University of New Mexico Press, 1952), 58–59.

21. William Clark to James Barbour, June 11, 1825, Documents Relating to the Negotiation of Ratified and Unratified Treaties with Various Tribes of Indians, 1801–1869, Introduction and Ratified Treaties, 1801–1826, RG75, Target 494, 1, National Archives and Records Administration; Unrau, *The Rise and Fall of Indian Country*, 42–43.

22. Kappler, *Treaties*, 246–250.

23. Cited in Stephen Sayles, "Thomas Hart Benton and the Santa Fe Trail," *Missouri Historical Review* 69, no. 1 (October 1974): 4–5.

24. Oliva, *Soldiers on the Santa Fe Trail*, 26.

25. Ibid., 25.

26. Ibid., 32–33.

27. Atkinson to William Bradford, December 15, 1819, and Atkinson to General Jacob Brown, November 23, 1825, cited in Nichols, *General Henry Atkinson*, 71, 109–110.

28. *U.S. Statutes at Large*, vol. 4: 35–36.

29. *U.S. Statutes at Large*, vol. 2: 141.

30. Kappler, *Treaties*, 252–254.

31. Ibid., passim, 262 ff.

32. Barry, *The Beginning of the West*, 121.

Chapter 4. Benton's Road

1. H. Craig Miner, *The St. Louis–San Francisco Transcontinental Railroad: The Thirty-fifth Parallel Project, 1853–1890* (Lawrence: University Press of Kansas, 1972), 17.

2. By A Senator of Thirty Years (Senator Thomas Hart Benton), *Thirty Years' View; or, A History of the Working of the American Government for Thirty Years*, vol. 1 (New York: Greenwood Press, 1968), 41.

3. Donald Chaput, *Francis X. Aubry: Trader, Trailmaker, and Voyageur in the Southwest, 1846–1854* (Glendale, CA: Arthur H. Clark Company, 1975), 44. See also Walker D. Wyman, "Freighting: A Big Business on the Santa Fe Trail," *Kansas Historical Quarterly* 1 (November 1931): 17–21.

4. *Santa Fe Republican*, November 13, 1847, cited in Chaput, *Francis X. Aubury*, 44.

5. John W. Steiger, "Benjamin O'Fallon," in LeRoy R. Hafen, ed., *The Mountain Men and the Fur Trade of the Far West*, vol. 5 (Glendale, CA: Arthur H. Clark Company, 1968), 263.

6. Benjamin O'Fallon to William Clark, December 15, 1824, Letters Received by the Office of Indian Affairs, St. Louis Superintendency, RG75, M234, R747, National Archives and Records Administration.

7. Benton, *Thirty Years' View*, 42.

8. Ibid., 42–43.

9. Ibid., 44; Sayles, *Thomas Hart Benton*, 14–15, 19; Andrés Reséndez, "Getting Cured and Getting Drunk: State vs. Market in Texas and New Mexico, 1800–1850," *Journal of the Early Republic* 22, no. 1 (Spring 2002): 95. There is some evidence that the Missouri memorial never arrived in Washington, as there is no clear record of its having been passed by both houses of the Missouri legislature. See Sayles, *Thomas Hart Benton*, 19.

10. Henry Nash Smith, *Virgin Land: The American West as Myth and Symbol* (Cambridge: Harvard University Press, 1978), 28–29; *Congressional Globe*, United States Senate, 29th Cong., 1st sess. (February 7, 1849), 473.

11. Morris F. Taylor, *First Mail West: Stagecoach Lines on the Santa Fe Trail* (Albuquerque: University of New Mexico Press, 1971) 1; Phillip D. Jordan, *The National Road* (New York: Bobbs-Merrill Company, 1948), 12–13.

12. Isenberg, "The Market Revolution," 464.

13. The Santa Trail: Communication from the Secretary of the Interior Transmitting the Final Report on the Addition of the Santa Fe Trail to the National Trails System, *House Document no. 189* (1977), 95th Cong., 1st sess. (Serial Set 13183), 28–29.

14. Santa Fe National Historic Trail, *House Report no. 240* (1987), 100th Cong., 1st sess. (Serial Set 13732), 2.

15. Henry Clay to Joel R. Poinsett, September 24, 1825, *American State Papers, Foreign Relations*, vol. 6, 581, cited in Henry P. Walker, *The Wagonmas-*

ters: High Plains Freighting from the Earliest Days of the Santa Fe Trail to 1880 (Norman: University of Oklahoma Press, 1966), 22.

16. *The Road to Santa Fe*, ed. Gregg, 1, 32; Barry, *Beginning of the West*, 122.

17. Jay H. Buckley, *William Clark, Diplomat* (Norman: University of Oklahoma Press, 2008), 157. Whether Clark's dispatch was sent by Chihuahuan authorities to Santa Fe or Taos is not known.

18. At a point a few miles northeast of present Clayton, New Mexico, Sibley and his crew saw what turned out to be the "Taos Gap" west of present Cimarron, New Mexico, through which they traveled en route to the Valley of Taos, which they reached on October 30, 1825. *The Road to Santa Fe*, ed. Gregg, 234, and David Dary, *The Santa Fe Trail: Its History, Legends & Lore* (New York: Penguin Books, 2002), 103–104.

19. Barry, *Beginning of the West*, 122–123; *The Road to Santa Fe*, ed. Gregg, 176.

20. Benton, *Thirty Years' View*, 43–44.

21. Walker, *The Wagonmasters*, 22.

22. Isenberg, "The Market Revolution," 462.

23. Hyslop, *Bound for Santa Fe*, 49.

24. Kappler, *Treaties*, 247.

25. *The Road to Santa Fe*, ed. Gregg, 58–59.

26. Benton, *Thirty Years' View*, 41.

27. Ibid., 44.

28. As late as 1905 the Kansas legislature appropriated $1,000 for the Daughters of the American Revolution to mark the "line of the Trail through the State" because the "ruts were filling in . . . and the true route was in danger of being forgotten." Kansas Day (January 29) of 1906 was designated "Trail Day" in the public schools, and the children were invited to contribute a penny each toward the fund, which resulted in another $584.40 for the setting of ninety-eight markers along the trail. See Anna E. Arnold, *A History of Kansas* (Topeka: State of Kansas, 1916), 216.

Chapter 5. Regulation Revisited

1. *U.S. Statutes at Large*, vol. 14: 280 (1866).

2. Prucha, *American Indian Policy*, 67.

3. *U.S. Statutes at Large*, vol. 4: 35 (1824).

4. Kappler, *Treaties*, 233.

5. *U.S. Statutes at Large*, vol. 2: 141 (1802).

6. Barry, *Beginning of the West*, 201.

7. Janet Lecompte, "Gantt's Fort and Bent's Picket Post," *Colorado Magazine* 41, no. 2 (Spring 1964): 111.

8. Entry 97, December 1, 1834, Abstract of Licenses, Letters Received by the Office of Indian Affairs, St. Louis Superintendency, RG75, M234, R749, National Archives and Records Administration.

9. Barry, *Beginning of the West*, 201.

10. *U.S. Statutes at Large*, vol. 2: 146 (1802).

11. Ibid., 3: 682–683 (1922).

12. Amos Stoddard, *Sketches, Historical and Descriptive of Louisiana* (Philadelphia: Matthew Carey, 1812), 444–445.

13. Richard Cummins to Elbert Herring, April 9, 1833, Letters Received by the Office of Indian Affairs, Fort Leavenworth Agency, RG75, M234, R300, National Archives and Records Administration.

14. Kappler, *Treaties*, 170–171, 304–305, 365–367, 376–377, 382–383.

15. Unrau, *White Man's Wicked Water*, 45.

16. Marston G. Clark to William Clark, September 30, 1833, Letters Received by the Office of Indian Affairs, St. Louis Superintendency, RG 75, M234, R750, National Archives and Records Administration.

17. Peter Way, "Evil Humors and Ardent Spirits: The Rough Culture of Canal Construction Workers," *Journal of American History* 79 (March 1993): 1412–1413.

18. William Clark to Lewis Cass, November 20, 1831, Letters Received by the Office of Indian Affairs, St. Louis Superintendency, M234, R749, National Archives and Records Administration.

19. Gary C. Stein, "A Fearful Drunkenness: The Liquor Trade to the Western Indians as Seen by European Travelers in America, 1800–1860," *Red River Valley Historical Review* 1 (Summer 1974): 110–111.

20. *U.S. Statutes at Large*, vol. 4: 564 (1834).

21. *U.S. Statutes at Large*, vol. 4: 729 (1834).

22. Private Council with the Delaware and Shawnee Chiefs, n.d., 1834, Letters Received by the Office of Indian Affairs, Western Superintendency, RG75, M234, R921, National Archives and Records Administration. The council may have been called by federal Indian Commissioners Montfort Stokes, John F. Schermerhorn, and Henry L. Elsworth and held at the Western Superintendent's headquarters near Fort Coffee and the Arkansas River in present eastern Oklahoma. See Edward E. Hill, *The Office of Indian Affairs, 1824–1880: Historical Sketches* (New York: Clearwater Publishing Company), 201.

Chapter 6. Benton Vindicated

1. *U.S. Statutes at Large*, vol. 4: 411–112 (1830).

2. *U.S. Statutes at Large*, vol. 4: 729–735 (1834).

3. Oliva, *Soldiers on the Santa Fe Trail*, 26; Barry, *Beginning of the West*, 146, 150–151. For a detailed but sometimes embellished account of the Indians' attack on the traders on the Cimarron (or dry) branch of the overland road in 1828, see Colonel Henry Inman, *The Old Santa Fe Trail: The Story of a Great Highway* (Topeka, KS: Crane and Company, 1899), 67–92.

4. Oliva, *Soldiers on the Santa Fe Trail*, 33.

5. Benton, *Thirty Years' View*, 42.

6. Socolofsky and Self, *Historical Atlas of Kansas*, Map 4. See also L. Dean Bark, *Rainfall Patterns in Kansas*, Kansas Agriculture Experiment Station Reprint No. 9 (Manhattan: Kansas Agriculture Experiment Station, 1961).

7. Benton, *Thirty Years' View*, 42.

8. Hämäläinen, *The Comanche Empire*, 164. It is worth noting also that on his return trip from New Mexico in 1822 William Becknell bought corn from the Kansa tribe. Barry, *Beginning of the West*, 97.

9. *U.S. Statutes at Large*, vol. 4: 729–733 (1834). As early as 1815 Congress passed a law making it illegal to "operate" a distillery in an ill-defined area called "Indian country," but with no mention of a penalty for breaking this law. See *U.S. Statutes at Large*, vol. 3: 243–244 (1815).

10. Unrau, *White Man's Wicked Water*, 31–33; Edward Broadhead, *Fort Pueblo* (Pueblo, CO: Pueblo County Historical Society, 1981), 4, 9; R. Richard Wohl, "Three Generations of Business Enterprise in a Midwestern City: The McGees of Kansas City," *Journal of Economic History* 16 (1956): 516–527; Richard Cummins to Elbert Herring, April 9, 1833, Letters Received by the Office of Indian Affairs, Fort Leavenworth Agency, RG75, M234, R300, National Archives and Records Administration.

11. Josiah Gregg, *Commerce of the Prairies,* 2 vols. (Ann Arbor, MI: University Microfilms, Inc., 1966), 332.

12. Barry, *The Beginning of the West*, 328, 413.

13. Ibid., p. 48.

14. W. J. Rorabaugh, *The Alcoholic Republic: An American Tradition* (New York: Oxford University Press, 1979), Table A1.2, 233.

15. Reséndez, "Getting Cured," 98.

16. Unrau, *White Man's Wicked Water*, 3.

17. For example, near Chicago in 1821, Michigan Indian Superintendent Lewis Cass was authorized by his superiors in the Indian Office to purchase

932 gallons of whiskey to facilitate passage of the Ottawa, Chippewa, and Potawatomi Treaty of August 21, 1821, see Bernard C. Peters, "Hypocrisy on the Great Lakes Frontier: The Use of Whiskey by the Michigan Department of Indian Affairs," *Michigan Historical Review* 18 (Fall 1992): 1–13. Four years later, under the direction of Secretary of War John C. Calhoun, the federal government spent $2,500 for whiskey in three months, amounting to $8.11 per day for each Choctaw delegate attending what turned out to be an abortive treaty conference in Washington. See Arthur H. DeRosier Jr., *The Removal of the Choctaw Indians* (Knoxville: University of Tennessee Press, 1970), 79–80, and Richard White, *The Roots of Dependency: Subsistence, Environment, and Social Change Among the Choctaws, Pawnees, and Navajos* (Lincoln: University of Nebraska Press, 1983), 121–122.

18. See, for example, David A. Dary, *The Buffalo Book: The Full Saga of the American Animal* (Chicago: Swallow Press, 1974), 74–75; David Lavender, *Bent's Fort* (Garden City, NY: Doubleday and Company, 1954), 149; Douglas C. Comer, *Ritual Ground: Bent's Old Fort, World Formation, and the Annexation of the Southwest* (Berkeley and Los Angeles: University of California Press, 1996), 115; David J. Weber, *The Taos Trappers: The Fur Trade of the Far Southwest, 1540–1846* (Norman: University of Oklahoma Press, 1971), passim; and Paul Chrisler Phillips, *The Fur Trade*, 2 vols. (Norman: University of Oklahoma Press, 1961), vol. 2: 527, 532.

19. Benton, *Thirty Years' View*, 42.

20. Kappler, *Treaties*, 595.

21. Ibid., 600.

22. Hämäläinen, *The Comanche Empire*, 165.

23. Marston G. Clark to William Clark, September 30, 1833, Letters Received by the Office of Indian Affairs, St. Louis Superintendency, RG75, M234, R750, National Archives and Records Administration; Rufus B. Sage, *Rocky Mountain Life; or Startling Scenes and Perilous Adventures in the Far West* (Dayton, OH: Edward Canby, 1846), 49, 354; Unrau, *White Man's Wicked Water*, 122.

24. John Montgomery to Alfred Cumming, August 31, 1855, Letters Received by the Office of Indian Affairs, Kansas Agency, RG75, M234, R364, National Archives and Records Administration.

25. Ibid.

26. Barry, *Beginning of the West*, 146; Report of William Clark, October 27, 1827, Letters Received by the Office of Indians Affairs, St. Louis Superintendency, RG75, M234, R748, National Archives and Records Administration.

27. George W. Ewing to James M. Porter, n.d., 1842, Letters Received by

the Office of Indian Affairs, St. Louis Superintendency, RG75, M234, R753, National Archives and Records Adminstration; Unrau, *The Kansa Indians*, 160.

28. Richard Cummins to Thomas Harvey, March 6, 1844, Letters Received by the Office of Indian Affairs, Fort Leavenworth Agency, RG75, M234, R302, National Archives and Records Administration.

29. Kappler, *Treaties*, 552–554.

30. Unrau, *The Kansa Indians*, 162–163.

31. Seth M. Hayes arrived at Council Grove in the summer of 1847 with instructions from the firm of Boone and Hamilton (his employers, who held a license to trade with the Kansa Indians) to establish a supply store "for the convenience of the overland freighters." By 1849 there were at least three or four shops in Council Grove and a least six log houses on the land only recently granted to the Kansas. Ibid., 165; Barry, *Beginning of the West*, 671.

32. Report of Richard Cummins, July 17, 1847, Letters Received by the Office of Indian Affairs, Fort Leavenworth Agency, RG75, M234, R302, National Archives and Records Administration.

Chapter 7. On the Upper Arkansas

1. Unrau, *The Kansa Indians*, 166; *U.S. Statutes at Large*, vol. 9: 203 (1847); Richard Cummins to Thomas Harvey, December 21. 1847, Letters Received by the Office of Indian Affairs, Fort Leavenworth Agency, RG75, M234, R302, National Archives and Records Administration.

2. Richard Cummins to Elbert Herring, April 9, 1833, Letters Received by the Office of Indian Affairs, Fort Leavenworth Agency, RG75, M234, R300, National Archives and Records Administration. Cummins's predecessor was George Vashon, who served as Delaware and Shawnee agent from April 15, 1829, to June 1, 1830. Vashon's initial trip from St. Louis to his new assignment was simply to make the Shawnee annuity payment near the mouth of the Kansas River, which took place on June 4, 1829, a little more than two months after his appointment. Soon thereafter he returned to St. Louis—perhaps within a week—and did not return to Indian Country until October 1829, at which time he issued a federal trade license to Francis G. Chouteau. See Hill, *Office of Indian Affairs*, 64–67; Barry, *Beginning of the West*, 156, 159.

3. Donald J. Berthrong, *The Southern Cheyennes* (Norman: University of Oklahoma Press, 1963), 4–21; Barry, *Beginning of the West*, 5; West, *The Contested Plains*, 68–70: Comer, *Ritual Ground*, 107–108.

4. West, *The Contested Plains*, 70–71.

5. John Whitfield to Alfred Cumming, August 15, 1855, Letters Received from the Office of Indian Affairs, August 15, 1855, Upper Arkansas Agency, RG75, M234, R878, National Archives and Records Administration, cited in Berthrong, *The Southern Cheyennes*, 132.

6. One historian flatly states: "Gantt, known as 'Baldhead' among the Cheyennes, introduced the tribe to whiskey on the Arkansas River." Berthrong, *The Southern Cheyennes*, 90. Another recounts that "during the winter of 1832–33 he [Gantt] traded with some Cheyennes and Arapahos [on the upper Arkansas near present Pueblo] for buffalo robes. By sweetening whiskey he persuaded these previously teetotaling Indians to drink it, thereby laying the foundation of the whiskey trade on the Arkansas." Janet Lecompte, *Pueblo, Hardscrabble, Greenhorn: The Upper Arkansas, 1832–1856* (Norman: University of Oklahoma Press, 1978), 10.

7. Lavender, *Bent's Fort*, 415.

8. John Dougherty to William Clark, November 10, 1831, Letters Received by the Office of Indian Affairs, St. Louis Superintendency, RG75, M234, R749, National Archives and Records Administration.

9. *The Journal of Jacob Fowler, Narrating an Adventure from Arkansas Through the Indian Territory, Oklahoma, Kansas, Colorado, and New Mexico, to the Sources of Rio Grande del Norte, 1821–1822*, ed. Elliott Coues (New York: Francis P. Harper, 1898), 58–59 (reprint, Fairfield, WA: Ye Gallen Press, 2000).

10. In the late eighteenth century the Spanish governor of Louisiana, Baron de Carondelet, considered the Cheyennes as some of the most canny traders of all the Indians he dealt with. Their meticulous quillwork on processed bison robes was well known and in much demand in the upper Platte and Black Hills country. Comer, *Ritual Ground*, 109.

11. Donald John Blakeslee, "The Plains Interband Trade System: An Ethnohistorical and Archeological Investigation," Ph.D. dissertation, Department of Anthropology, University of Wisconsin-Milwaukee, 1975, cited in Comer, *Ritual Ground*, 110–111; *The Journal of Jacob Fowler*, 58–59; Barry, *The Beginning of the West*, 97.

12. According to topographical engineer William H. Emory, Big Timbers was a large grove of cottonwood trees about a mile in width along the northern bank of the Arkansas, midway between present Las Animas and Lamar, Colorado. Berthrong, *The Southern Cheyennes*, 98, n. 36.

13. Lavender, *Bent's Fort*, 149. By about 1838 the beaver trade began to recover, especially in areas where the reproductive capacity of the animals was encour-

aged by the fewer number of trappers working the tributaries of the upper Rio Grande, Arkansas, and South Platte. See Phillips, *The Fur Trade*, vol. 2, 532.

14. Comer, *Ritual Ground*, 204; David Fridtjof Halaas and Andrew E. Masich, *Halfbreed: The Remarkable True Story of George Bent—Caught Between the Worlds of the Indian and the White Man* (Cambridge, MA: Da Capo Press, paperback edition, 2005), 1.

15. George E. Hyde, *Life of George Bent Written from His Letters*, ed. Savoie Lottinville (Norman: University of Oklahoma Press, 1967), 60–61, n. 7.

16. On July 4, 1825, Charles Bent, Joshua Pilcher, Lucien Fontenelle, William Vanderburgh, and Andrew Drips (successors to the old Missouri Fur Company) were granted a federal license to trade with Indians "at the mouth of the Kansas river." Barry, *The Beginning of the West*, 125.

17. Ibid., 173.

18. Comer, *Ritual Ground*, 92, 200–203.

19. Lavender, *Bent's Fort*, 138–140; Halaas and Masich, *Halfbreed*, 9; West, *The Contested Plains*, 83; Lecompte, *Pueblo, Hardscrabble, Greenhorn*, 10.

20. Barry, *The Beginning of the West*, 222, 233; Comer, *Ritual Ground*, 204; John Dougherty to William Clark, November 10, 1831, Letters Received by the Office of Indian Affairs, St. Louis Superintendency, RG75, M234, R749, National Archives and Records Administration.

21. Comer, *Ritual Ground*, 206, says "about 1829"; Halaas and Masich, *Halfbreed*, 9–10, opt for about 1830; Lavender, *Bent's Fort*, 138–139, is unclear but seems to prefer 1831; Savoie Lottinville in Hyde, *Life of George Bent*, 60–61, n. 7, argues for an "uncertain [time] but after John Gantt's post was built on the upper Arkansas in 1832."

22. Halaas and Masich, *Halfbreed*, 9–10, 19–24.

23. Comer, *Ritual Ground*, 123; Berthrong, *The Southern Cheyennes*, 24–26; Lavender, *Bent's Fort*, 142.

24. William Gordon to William Clark, October 3, 1831, William Clark Papers, Kansas State Historical Society, vol. 6, 301, cited in Berthrong, *The Southern Cheyennes*, 24.

25. Comer, *Ritual Trade*, 154–155.

26. *U.S. Statutes at Large*, vol. 4: 729–735 (1834).

27. Francis Paul Prucha, *The Great Father: The United States Government and the American Indians*, 2 vols. (Lincoln: University of Nebraska Press, 1984), vol. 1, 132.

Chapter 8. Tribal Annuities and Bison Robes

1. Kickapoos to Commissioner Ellsworth, September(?) 1833, Letters Received by the Office of Indian Affairs, Western Superintendency, RG75, M234, R921, National Archives and Records Administration.

2. Ellsworth Talk with Kickapoos, in ibid.

3. *U.S. Statutes at Large*, vol. 4: 733 (1834).

4. William Clark to Lewis Cass, November 20, 1831, Letters Received by the Office of Indian Affairs, St. Louis Superintendency, RG75, M234, R749, National Archives and Records Administration.

5. For a general study of alcohol regulation and prohibition in Indian Country, see Unrau, *White Man's Wicked Water.*

6. Willard Carl Klunder, *Lewis Cass and the Politics of Moderation* (Kent, OH: Kent State University Press, 1996), 52.

7. Lewis Cass, "Remarks on the Policy and Practices of the United States and Great Britain in Their Treatment of the Indian," *North American Review* 24 (1827): 404–405. Cass became secretary of war on August 1, 1831.

8. Gary C. Stein, "A Fearful Drunkenness: The Liquor Trade to the Western Indians as Seen by European Travelers in America, 1800–1860," *Red River Valley Historical Review* 1 (Summer 1974): 110–111.

9. *U.S. Statutes at Large*, vol. 2: 146 (1802).

10. Rorabaugh, *The Alcoholic Republic*, table A1.2, 233.

11. *U.S. Statutes at Large*, vol. 3: 243–244 (1815).

12. Ibid., vol. 3, 683–683 (1822).

13. *U.S. Statutes at Large*, vol. 4: 564 (1832).

14. For Senator Benton's involvement with the American Fur Company's problems with illegal alcohol in Indian Country, see Unrau, *White Man's Wicked Water*, 67–69, and Deposition of John A. Sire in *United States v. Alexander Culbertson*, United States District Circuit Court for the District of Missouri, April 1848 Term, copy in Letters Received by the Office of Indian Affairs, RG75, M234, R755, National Archives and Records Administration.

15. Pierre Chouteau to David D. Mitchell, August 23, 1842, Letters Received by the Office of Indian Affairs, St. Louis Superintendency, RG75, M234, R753, National Archives and Records Administration.

16. William E. Miller, *History of Jackson County* (Kansas City, MO: Birdsall and Williams, 1881), 70.

17. Kappler, *Treaties*, 519–524, 531–534.

18. Ibid., passim.

19. Lewis E. Atherton, "James and Robert Aull—A Frontier Mercantile Firm," *Missouri Historical Review* 30, no. 1 (October 1935): 3–9.

20. Rufus B. Sage, *Rocky Mountain Life; or, Startling Scenes and Perilous Adventures in the Far West* (Dayton, OH: Edward Canby, 1846), 52.

21. Unrau, *White Man's Wicked Water*, 52.

22. Ibid., 54.

23. Richard Cummins to Thomas Harvey, January 20, 1848, Letters Received by the Office of Indian Affairs, Fort Leavenworth Agency, RG75, M234, R301, National Archives and Records Administration.

24. Petition of David Waldo, James Brown, John J. Johns, ? Reid, Jaboz Smith, William McCoy, and William Gilpin to President of the United States, January 10, 1851, Letters Received by the Office of Indian Affairs, Osage River Agency, RG75, M234, R644, National Archives and Records Administration.

25. *Kansas Press* (Council Grove), October 10, 1859.

26. Joseph Street to (?), n.d., *Annual Report of the Commissioner of Indian Affairs* (1838), cited in Unrau, *The Rise and Fall of Indian Country*, 106; Barry, *Beginning of the West*, 1181.

27. D. D. Mitchell to T. Hartley Crawford, September 19, 1843, *Annual Report of the Commissioner of Indian Affairs* (1843), NCR 872, R4158, 386–387.

28. Kappler, *Treaties*, 594–595, 600–601.

29. Richard Cummins to Thomas Harvey, December 21, 1847, Letters Received by the Office of Indian Affairs, Fort Leavenworth Agency, RG75, M234, R302, National Archives and Records Administration.

30. Barry, *Beginning of the West*, 626.

31. Sondra Van Meter, *Marion County Kansas: Past and Present* (Marion, KS: Marion County Historical Society, 1972), 21–25: Unrau, *White Man's Wicked Water*, 47–48, 62–66. For the involvement of the Kiowas, Comanches, and other southern Plains tribes in the alcohol market at Walnut Creek and the surrounding Great Bend area, see Jesse Leavenworth to Dennis Cooley, March 26 and May 8, 1866, and H. R. Mead to Thomas Murphy, September 7, 1866, Kiowa-Comanche Agency, RG75, M234, R375, National Archives and Records Administration; Henry M. Stanley, *My Early Travels in American and Asia* (London: Gerald Duckworth and Co., 2001), 92, 240–241; Oliva, *Soldiers on the Santa Fe Trail*, 143, 147; and Louise Barry, "The Ranch at Walnut Creek Crossing," *Kansas Historical Quarterly* 37, no. 2 (Summer 1971): 121–147.

32. Berthrong, *The Southern Cheyennes*, 24–25; Halaas and Masich, *Halfbreed*, 10–11.

33. Ibid., 6–10.

34. See, for example, Lavender, *Bent's Fort*, 140–142.

35. George Bird Grinnell, "Bent's Old Fort and Its Builders," *Collections of the Kansas State Historical Society* 15 (1919–1922): 31.

36. Berthrong, *The Southern Cheyennes*, 24.

37. Barry, *Beginning of the West*, 160, 233.

38. Oliva, *Soldiers on the Santa Fe Trail*, 33–34.

39. Pekka Hämäläinen, "The Western Comanche Trade Center: Rethinking the Plains Indian Trade System," *Western Historical Quarterly* 29, no. 4 (Winter 1998): 506, 511–512.

40. "Hugh Evans' Journal of Colonel Henry Dodge's Expedition to the Rocky Mountains in 1835," ed. Fred S. Perrine, *Mississippi Valley Historical Review* 14, no. 2 (September 1927): 211–212.

41. In 1836, distiller and alcohol trader Simon Turley at Arroyo Hondo (a few miles north of Taos) hired Charles Autobee to take flour and whiskey to market on the Arkansas, to a point near the mouth of Fountain Creek. Broadhead, *Fort Pueblo*, 9.

42. Agent John Dougherty reported in 1831 that 2,200 packs (or bales) of bison robes had been purchased in the upper Missouri country for whiskey. Dougherty to William Clark, November 10, 1831, Letters Received by the Office of Indian Affairs, St. Louis Superintendency, RG75, M234, R749, National Archives and Records Administration.

43. Lecompte, "Gantt's Fort," 119.

44. Haalas and Masich, *Halfbreed*, 10.

45. George P. Hammond, *The Adventures of Alexander Barclay, Mountain Man* (Denver, CO: Old West Publishing Company, 1976), 25, 49, 46, 70.

46. *The Life and Adventures of James P. Beckworth as Told to Thomas D. Bonner* (Lincoln: University of Nebraska Press), 436.

47. *U.S. Statutes at Large*, vol. 7: 203 (1847).

Chapter 9. Trade Alcohol

1. Dan Flores, "Bison Ecology and Bison Diplomacy: The Southern Plains from 1800 to 1850," *Journal of American History* 78, no. 2 (September 1991): 483.

2. Andrew C. Isenberg, *The Destruction of the Bison: An Environmental History, 1750–1920* (New York: Cambridge University Press, 2000), 98, 100; Berthrong, *The Southern Cheyennes*, 36.

3. Barry, *The Beginning of the West*, 257.

4. Weber, *The Taos Traders*, 212; Gard, *The Buffalo Hunters*, 57.

5. West, *The Contested Plains*, 76–77; Comer, *Ritual Ground*, 124–125; Berthrong, *The Southern Cheyennes*, 82–84; Brian Delay, *War of a Thousand Deserts: Indian Raids and the U.S.-Mexican War* (New Haven: Yale University Press, 2008), 80–81; Sage, *Rocky Mountain Life*, 52.

6. Broadhead, *Fort Pueblo*, 9.

7. Elinor Wilson, *Jim Beckworth: Black Mountain Man and War Chief of the Crows* (Norman: University of Oklahoma Press, 1955), 39.

8. David D. Mitchell to T. Hartley Crawford, September 29, 1843, *Annual Report of the Commissioner of Indian Affairs for 1843*, 388.

9. Joseph J. Gallagher et al., Historic Resources of the Santa Fe Trail, 1821–1880, Report to United States Department of the Interior, National Park Service, 1994, http://pdfhost.focus.nps.gov/docs/NRHP/Text/64500224.pdf, 6 (accessed December 14, 2009).

10. Bent's Old Fort National Historic Site, "A Self-Guiding Tour," National Park Service, U.S. Department of the Interior, n.d., n.p.

11. C. C. Hutchinson to H. B. Branch, September 17, 1862, *Annual Report of the Commissioner of Indian Affairs* (1862), NCR Reprint 872, R4158, 108.

12. *The Life and Adventures of James P. Beckworth as Told to Thomas D. Bonner*, Introduction and Notes by Delmont R. Oswald (Lincoln: University of Nebraska Press, 1972), 433–434.

13. Isenberg, *The Destruction of the Bison*, 104, 107.

14. Edward Lagrand Sabin, *Kit Carson Days (1809–1868)* (Chicago: A. C. McClurg & Co., 1914), 108.

15. The Ranch at Walnut Creek was established by William Allison and Francis Boothe in 1855, primarily to trade with the Kiowas and Comanches. The following year Allison brought 10,000 dried bison tongues and numerous bison robes, indicating that the operation was a success. Travelers on the overland road reported that "poor whiskey" was always available at Walnut Creek, and in early 1866 the Indian Office obtained a military order to close the ranch for whiskey violations, but to no avail. The operator at the time, Charles Rath, claimed the ranch was on the overland road that was not in Indian Country, see Louis Barry, "The Ranch at Walnut Creek," *Kansas Historical Quarterly* 37, no. 2 (Summer 1971): 123–124, 127–129, 139–142.

16. Barry, *The Beginning of the West*, 671–672.

17. James Hobbs, *Wild Life in the Far West; Personal Adventures of a Border Man*, facsimile reprint of the 1872 ed. (Alexandria, VA: Time-Life Books, 1980), 51, 101–102.

18. Halaas and Masich, *Halfbreed*, 23–26.

19. Ida Ellen Rath, *The Rath Trail* (Wichita, KS: McCormick-Armstrong Co., Inc., 1961), 9. Available at http://www.kancoll.org/books/rath/ (accessed January 12, 2010).

20. *Revised Statutes of the United States, Passed at the First Session of the Forty-Third Congress, 1873–1874* (Washington, DC: Government Printing Office, 1875), 375.

21. Marston G. Clark to William Clark, September 30, 1833, Letters Received by the Office of Indian Affairs, St. Louis Superintendency, RG75, M234, R750, National Archives and Records Administration.

22. Richard Cummins to Elbert Herring, April 9, 1833, Letters Received by the Office of Indian Affairs, Fort Leavenworth Agency, RG75, M234, R300, National Archives and Records Administration.

23. Sage, *Rocky Mountain Life*, 49.

24. *Kansas Press* (Council Grove), October 10, 1859, and *Western Journal of Commerce* (Kansas City, MO), August 23, 1860, cited in Unrau, *White Man's Wicked Water*, 85, 122.

25. Unrau, *The Kansa Indians*, 198.

26. William E. Unrau, "The Depopulation of the Dheghia-Siouan Kansa Prior to Removal," *New Mexico Historical Review* 48, no. 4 (1973): 320.

27. Commanding Officer Fort Leavenworth to B. A. James, August 8, 1853, of Indian Affairs, and Richard Cummins to Elbert Herring, April 9, 1833, Letters Received by the Office of Indian Affairs, Fort Leavenworth Agency, RG75, M234, R300, R733, National Archives and Records Administration.

28. D. D. Mitchell to T. Hartley Crawford, September 29, 1843, *Annual Report of the Commissioner of Indian Affairs* (1843), 388.

29. John Chambers to T. Hartley Crawford, September 27, 1844, *Annual Report of the Commissioner of Indian Affairs* (1844), NCR Reprint 872, R4158, 115, 135.

30. Thomas Fitzpatrick to T. Hartley Crawford, September 18, 1847, *Annual Report of the Commissioner of Indian Affairs* (1847), NCR Reprint 872, R4158, 125–129.

31. Ibid., 115.

32. Peter J. Powell, *Sweet Medicine: The Continuing Role of the Sacred Arrows, the Sun Dance, and the Sacred Buffalo Hat in Northern Cheyenne History*, 2 vols. (Norman: University of Oklahloma Press, 1969), 45; Halaas and Masich, *Halfbreed*, 30.

33. Lewis H. Garrard, *Wah-To-Yah and the Taos Trail* (Norman: University of Oklahoma Press, 1955), 76–77.

34. Unrau, *White Man's Wicked Water*, 45.

35. Kappler, *Treaties*, 594–595.

36. On December 13, 1834, Charles Bent for Bent, St. Vrain & Co. was granted a two-year Indian trade license for several upper Arkansas locations—including "Fort William [Bent's Fort] on the north side of the Arkansas about 40 miles east [*sic*] of the Rocky Mts.," which was well within the legal boundaries of Indian Country at that time. See Barry, *The Beginning of the West*, 257, and *U.S. Statutes at Large*, vol. 3: 682–683 (1822).

37. Cited in Leroy R. and Ann W. Hafen, eds., *Relations with the Indians of the Plains, 1857–1861: A Documentary Account*, in vol. 9 of *The Far West and Rockies Series*, ed. Leroy R. Hafen (Glendale, CA: Arthur H. Clark Company, 1959), 43.

38. Halaas and Masich, *Halfbreed*, 30.

39. Thomas Fitzpatrick to Thomas Harvey, September 18, 1847, *Annual Report of the Commissioner of Indian Affairs* (1847), 128–129.

40. "W. M. Boggs Manuscript about Bent's Fort, Kit Carson, the Far West and Life among the Indians," *Colorado Magazine* 7 (March 1930): 51; Barry, *The Beginning of the West*, 548, 641–642.

41. Halaas and Masich, *Halfbreed*, xiv.

42. George Bird Grinnell, "Bent's Old Fort and Its Builder," *Collections of the Kansas State Historical Society* 15 (1919–1922): 59.

43. Barry, *The Beginning of the West*, 968.

44. Ibid., 1117.

45. Oliva, *Soldiers on the Santa Fe Trail*, 143.

46. Kappler, *Treaties*, 600–602.

47. Barry, "The Ranch at Walnut Creek," 121–123, 127–129, 139–142; Stanley, *My Early Travels*, 36; Rath, *The Rath Trail*, 4–5.

48. Rath, *The Rath Trail*, 5.

49. Benton, *Thirty Years' View*, 42.

50. *U.S. Statutes at Large*, vol. 14: 230 (1866).

Chapter 10. Roads Unregulated

1. Oliva, *Soldiers on the Santa Fe Trail*, 25.

2. Frazer, *Forts of the West*, 39–40, 50–56, 59, 105–106.

3. Oliva, *Soldiers on the Santa Fe Trail*, 167–168.

4. Ibid., 108–110, 130.

5. *U.S. Statutes at Large*, vol. 9: 203 (1847).

6. Robert A. Trennert Jr., *Alternative to Extinction: Federal Indian Policy*

and the Beginnings of the Reservation System (Philadelphia: Temple University Press, 1976), 27.

7. Ibid., 106–107; Oliva, *Soldiers on the Santa Fe Trail*, 91.

8. Barry, *The Beginning of the West*, 574.

9. Thomas L. Karnes, "Gilpin's Volunteers on the Santa Fe Trail," *Kansas Historical Quarterly* 30, no. 2 (September 1962): 2, 7.

10. George Douglas Brewerton, *Overland with Kit Carson: A Narrative of the Old Spanish Trail in '48* (New York: A. L. Burt Company, 1930), 3, 258.

11. H. P. Bennet to William P. Dole, January 28, 1864, *Annual Report of the Commissioner of Indian Affairs* (1864), 245; Unrau, *White Man's Wicked Water*, 47.

12. Robert A. Trennert Jr., "Indian Policy on the Santa Fe Road: The Fitzpatrick Controversy of 1847–1848," *Kansas History* 1, no. 4 (Winter 1978), 250–151. The conflict between Agent Fitzpatrick and Colonel Gilpin over civilian versus military control over Indian affairs was by no means unique, especially after administration of federal Indian policy was transferred from the War Department to the newly established Interior Department in 1849. See, for example, William E. Unrau, "Indian Agent v. the Army: Some Background Notes on the Kiowa-Comanche Treaty of 1865," *Kansas Historical Quarterly* 30, no. 2 (Summer 1962): 129–152; and Donald J. D'Elia, "Argument Over Civilian or Military Control, 1865–1880," *The Historian* 24 (February 1962).

13. D'Elia, "Argument Over Civilian or Military Control, 1865–1880"; Richard Cummins to Thomas Harvey, February 27, 1848, Letters Received by the Office of Indian Affairs, Fort Leavenworth Agency, RG75, M234, R302, National Archives and Records Administration.

14. Records of the District Courts of the United States, District of Missouri, Complete and Final Returns (1848), United States Circuit Court, RG21, Federal Records Center, Kansas City, Missouri.

15. Gen'l. L. Jones, AGO, to William Medill, February 8, 1848, Letters Received by the Office of Indian Affairs, Fort Leavenworth Agency, RG75, M234, R302, National Archives and Records Administration.

16. Richard Cummins to Thomas Harvey, December 21, 1847, Letters Received by the Office of Indian Affairs, Fort Leavenworth Agency, RG75, M234, R302, National Archives and Records Administration.

17. Ibid.

18. Cummins explained further: "This laudable change in their business has not emanated from a regard for the law, nor from philanthropic motives, but from the fact of it becoming a nuisance, and very dangerous to those having large investments in the trade, and whose expenses were heavy; and not being able to compete successfully with the numerous small traders who infest

this country, and whose expenses are comparatively nothing—whose whole stock in trade amounted to only a few trinkets and three or four hundred gallons of liquor, procured on the Missouri frontier, New Mexico, or Hudson Bay," in Thomas Fitzpatrick to Thomas H. Harvey, September 18, 1847, *Annual Report of the Commissioner of Indian Affairs* (1847), NCR 872, R4158, 128–129.

19. Richard Cummins to Thomas Harvey, December 21, 1847, January 20, 27, 1848, Letters Received by the Office of Indian Affairs, Fort Leavenworth Agency, RG75, M234, R301, 302, National Archives and Records Administration.

20. For Comanche moderation in the use of alcohol during the first half of the nineteenth century, see Hämäläien, "The Western Comanche Trade Center," 511, and Delay, *War of a Thousand Deserts*, 101–103, 364.

21. Charles N. Handy to David D. Mitchell, September 6, 1850, *Annual Report of the Commissioner of Indian Affairs* (1850), NCR Reprint 872, R4158.

22. Thomas Fitzpatrick to Alfred Cumming, September 19, 1853, *Annual Report of the Commissioner of Indian Affairs* (1853), NCR Reprint 872, R4158.

23. Barry, *The Beginning of the West*, 124. The state legislature extended such designation of the road to the western Kansas border in 1868. Ibid.

24. Robert Smith Bader, *Prohibition in Kansas: A History* (Lawrence: University Press of Kansas, 1986), 20–21. It is interesting to note that some members of the territorial legislature chose to board at Westport, Missouri, a few miles east; because federal law banned alcohol at the Shawnee Mission, the situation was "not wholly satisfactory to those who needed stimulation produced by the spirit of corn." Ibid.

25. Barry, "The Ranch at Walnut Creek," 121; Oliva, *Soldiers on the Santa Fe Trail*, 143.

26. Walker, *The Wagonmasters*, 185.

27. Jesse H. Leavenworth to Dennis N. Cooley, May 8, 1866, Letters Received by the Office of Indian Affairs, Kiowa-Comanche Agency, RG75, M234, R375, National Archives and Records Administration.

28. The Grimes amendment to the Trade and Intercourse Law of 1866, *Congressional Globe* (March 19, 1866), 149.

29. *Bates v. Clark*, 95 U.S. 204 (1877).

30. Kappler, *Treaties*, 247, 249.

31. An assessment of these evasions is in Unrau, *White Man's Wicked Water*, 58–78.

32. A not atypical example of the difficulty of prosecuting violators came in 1847. It involved one Abraham Potter for selling whiskey to Indians some-

where in Indian Country and was filed in a Missouri federal court on July 2, 1847. For reasons not recorded it was continued to March 3, 1853, at which time it was again continued "because the defendant could not be found." In late July 1854, the *Potter* case was finally dismissed on grounds that "the witness have all disappeared." See United States District Attorney Reports-Returns, Entry 145, vol. 3, Missouri–North Carolina (1851–1856), RG206, National Archives and Records Administration.

33. Prucha, *American Indian Policy*, 275–277.

34. H. Craig Miner and William E. Unrau, *The End of Indian Kansas: A Study of Cultural Revolution, 1854–1871* (Lawrence: Regents Press of Kansas, 1978), 55–56.

35. Oliva, *Soldiers of the Santa Fe Trail*, 106, 108–109.

Bibliography

Unpublished Government Records

Deposition of John A. Sire in *United States v. Alexander Culbertson*, in United States District Court for the District of Missouri, April 1848 Term, copy in Letters Received by the Office of Indian Affairs, RG75, M234, R755, National Archives and Records Administration.

Documents Relating to the Negotiation of Ratified and Unratified Treaties with the Various Tribes of Indians, 1801–1869, Introduction and Ratified Treaties, RG75, T494, National Archives and Records Administration.

Letters Received by the Office of Indian Affairs, Fort Leavenworth Agency, RG75, M234, R300-303, National Archives and Administration.

Letters Received by the Office of Indian Affairs, Kansas Agency, RG75, M234, R364-367, National Archives and Records Administration.

Letter Received by the Office of Indian Affairs, Kiowa-Comanche Agency, RG75, M234, R375-37, National Archives and Records Administration.

Letters Received by the Office of Indian Affairs, Osage River Agency, RG75, M234, R642-644, National Archives and Records Administration.

Letters Received by the Office of Indian Affairs, St. Louis Superintendency, RG75, M234, R747-756, National Archives and Records Administration.

Letters Received by the Office of Indian Affairs, Upper Arkansas Agency, RG 75, M234, R878-879, National Archives and Administration.

Letters Received by the Office of Indian Affairs, Western Superintendency, RG921-923, M234, R922-923, National Archives and Records Administration.

"A Map Exhibiting the Territorial Limits of the Several Indian Nations and Tribes Agreeable to the notes of A. Chouteau, reduced & laid down on a scale of 80 miles to an inch, By R. Paul, February 1816." RG75, Cartographic Branch, Map 884, Tube 702, National Archives and Records Administration.

Map of the State of Kansas, Compiled chiefly from the official records of the United States General Office, with supplemental data from other map making agencies, under the direction of L. P. Berthrong, Chief of the Drafting Division, G. L. O., 1925, *Kansas or Kaw Indians vs. United States* (Court of Claims F-64), June 1, 1932, RG75, Map 11321, Tube 1387, Cartographic Branch, National Archives and Records Administration.

Records of the District Courts of the United States, District of Missouri, Complete and Final Returns (1848), United States Circuit Court, RG21, Federal Records Center, Kansas City.

United States District Attorney Reports-Returns, entry 145, vol. 3, Missouri-North Carolina (1851–1856), RG206, National Archives and Records Administration.

Published Government Records

American State Papers, vol. 2: *Indian Affairs*. Washington, DC: Gales and Seaton, 1832–1834.

Annual Reports of the Commissioner of Indian Affairs (1834–1853). NCR Reprint 872, R4158.

Carter, Clarence E., comp. and ed. *The Territorial Papers of the United States*. 26 vols. Washington, DC: Government Printing Office, 1934–1962.

Congressional Globe, 31st Cong., 2nd Sess. (1850), and 33rd Cong., 2nd Sess. (1854).

Kappler, Charles J., comp. *Indian Affairs: Law and Treaties*. 5 vols. Washington, DC: Government Printing Office, 1904.

Royce, Charles C. *Indian Land Cessions in the United States*. Eighteenth Annual Report of the Bureau of American Ethnology, 1896–1897, part 2. Washington, DC: Government Printing Office, 1899.

Santa Fe National Historical Trail, *House Report no. 240* (1987), 100th Cong., 1st Sess. (Serial 13732), 2.

The Santa Fe Trail: Communication from the Secretary of the Interior Transmitting the Final Report on the Additions of the Santa Fe Trail to the National Trails System, *House Document no. 189* (1977), 95th Cong., 1st Sess. (Serial 131183), 28–29.

U.S. Statutes at Large, vol. 2 (1802), 3 (1815, 1822), 4 (1832, 1834), 9 (1847), and 14 (1866).

Manuscripts and Newspapers

George C. Sibley Papers, Manuscript Division, Missouri Historical Society, St. Louis.

Second Colorado Regiment Veterans Papers. Manuscript Division, State Historical Society of Colorado, Denver.

Niles Weekly Register (Baltimore).

Western Journal of Commerce (City of Kansas [Kansas City]).

Online Sources

Bevins, Charles I., ed. "Adams-Onis Treaty of 1819." *Treaties and other International Agreements of the United States of America, 1776–1949*, Wallace L. Mckeehan 1997–2001, vol. 2, http://www.tamu.edu/ccbn/dewitt/adamonis.htm (accessed July 7, 2010).

Gallagher, Joseph J., et al, Historic Resources of the Santa Fe Trail, 1821–1880, Report to United States Department of Interior, National Park Service, http://pdfhost.focus.nps.gov.docs/NRHP/Text/64500224.pdf, 6 (accessed March 4, 2010).

Olson, Michael L., and Harry C. Meyers. "The Diary of Pedro Ignacio Gallego Wherein 400 Soldiers Following the Trail of the Comanches Met by William Becknell on His First Trip to Santa Fe." *Best of Wagon Tracks* 7, no. 1 (November 1992), n.p., http://www.santafetrail.org/wagontracks DIARY-OF-PEDRO-IGNACIO-GALLEGO.pdf (accessed January 14, 2010).

Rath, Ida Ellen. *The Rath Trail* 9, (Wichita: McCormick-Armstrong Co., Inc.), http://www.kancoll.org/books/rath/ (accessed March 21, 2010).

Books and Journal Articles

Arnold, Anna E. *A History of Kansas*. Topeka: State of Kansas, 1931.

Athearn, Frederick J. *A Forgotten Empire: The Spanish Frontier in Colorado and New Mexico, 1540–1821*. Denver: Bureau of Land Management, Denver Office, 1989.

Atherton, Lewis E. "James and Robert Aull—A Frontier Mercantile Firm." *Missouri Historical Review* 30, no. 1 (October 1935).

Bader, Robert Smith. *Prohibition in Kansas: A History*. Lawrence: University Press of Kansas, 1986.

Bannon, John Francis. *The Spanish Borderlands Frontier, 1513–1821*. New York: Holt, Rinehart and Winston, 1970.

Bark, L. Dean. *Rainfall Patterns in Kansas, Kansas Agriculture Experiment Station Reprint no. 9*. Manhattan: Kansas Agriculture Experiment Station, 1961.

Barry, Louise. *The Beginning of the West: Annals of the Kansas Gateway to the American West, 1540–1854*. Topeka: Kansas State Historical Society, 1972.

———. "The Ranch at Walnut Creek." *Kansas Historical Quarterly* 37, no. 2 (Summer 1971).

Beachum, Larry. *William Becknell, Father of the Santa Fe Trail*. El Paso: Texas Western Press, 1982.

Benton, Thomas Hart. ("By a Senator of Thirty Years," Senator Thomas Hart Benton). *Thirty Years' View: or, A History of the Working of the American Government for Thirty Years*, vol. 1. New York: Greenwood Press, 1968.

Berthrong, Donald J. *The Southern Cheyennes*. Norman: University of Oklahoma Press, 1963.

Billington, Ray Allen. *Western Expansion: A History of the American Frontier*. New York: Macmillan Company, 3rd ed., 1967.

Blakeslee, Donald J. *Along Ancient Trails: The Mallet Expedition of 1739*. Niwot: University Press of Colorado, 1995.

Boggs, W. M. "Manuscript About Bent's Fort, Kit Carson, the Far West, and Life Among the Indians." *Colorado Magazine* 7, no. 2 (March 1930).

Brewerton, George Douglas, *Overland with Kit Carson: A Narrative of the Old Spanish Trail*. New York: A. L. Burt, 1930.

Broadhead, Edward. *Fort Pueblo*. Pueblo, CO: Pueblo County Historical Society, 1981.

Buckley, Jay H. *William Clark, Diplomat*. Norman: University of Oklahoma Press, 2008.

Bushnell, David I. Jr. "Villages of the Algonqian, Siouan and Caddoan Tribes West of the Mississippi." Bureau of American Ethnology *Bulletin* 77 (1927).

Chalfant, William Y. *Dangerous Passage: The Santa Fe Trail and the Mexican War*. Norman: University of Oklahoma Press, 1994.

Chambers, William Nisbet. *Old Bullion Benton, Senator from the New West, 1782–1858*. Boston: Little, Brown and Company, 1956.

Chaput, Donald. *Francis X. Aubry: Trader, Trailmaker, and Voyageur in the Southwest, 1846–1854*. Glendale, CA: Arthur H. Clark Company, 1975.

Cleland, Robert Glass. *This Reckless Breed of Men: The Trappers and Fur Traders of the Southwest.* New York: Alfred A. Knopf, 1963.

Comer, Douglas C. *Ritual Ground: Bent's Fort, World Formation, and the Annexation of the Southwest.* Berkeley and Los Angeles: University of California Press, 1996.

Coues, Elliott, ed. *The Journal of Jacob Fowler, Narrating an Adventure from Arkansas Through the Indian Territory, Oklahoma, Kansas, Colorado, and New Mexico.* New York: Francis P. Harper, 1898, reprint, Fairfield, Washington, DC: Ye Gallen Press, 2000.

Dary, David. *The Santa Fe Trail: Its History, Legends, and Lore.* New York: Penguin Books, 2002.

Delay, Brian. *War of a Thousand Deserts: Indian Raids and the U.S.-Mexican War.* New Haven: Yale University Press, 2008.

D'Elia, Donald J. "Argument over Civilian or Military Control, 1865–1880." *The Historian* 24 (February 1962).

Flores, Dan. "Bison Ecology and Bison Diplomacy: The Southern Plains from 1800 to 1850." *Journal of American History* 78, no. 2 (September 1991).

Ford, Paul Leicester, ed. *The Works of Thomas Jefferson*, vol. 10. New York: G. P. Putnam's Sons, 1905.

Franzwa, Gregory M. *Maps of the Santa Fe Trail.* St. Louis: Patrice Press, 1989.

Frazer, Robert W. *Fort of the West: Military Forts and Presidos and Posts Commonly Called Forts West of the Mississippi to 1898.* Norman: University of Oklahoma Press, 1965.

Gard, Wayne. *The Great Buffalo Hunt.* New York: Alfred A.. Knopf, 1959.

Garrard, Lewis H. *Wah-To-Yah and the Taos Trail.* Norman: University of Oklahoma Press, 1955.

Glaab, Charles N. "Business Patterns in the Growth of a Midwestern City: The Kansas City Business Community before the Civil War." *Business History Review* 33, no. 2 (Summer 1959).

Goetzmann, William H. *Exploration and Empire: The Exporer and Scientist in the Winning of the American West.* New York: Alfred A. Knopf, 1966.

Gregg, Kate L., ed. *The Road to Santa Fe: The Journal and Diaries of George Champlin Sibley Pertaining to the Surveying and Marking of a Road from the Missouri Frontier to the Settlements of New Mexico.* Albuquerque: University of New Mexico Press, 1951.

Grinnell, George Bird. "Bent's Fort and Its Builders." *Collections of the Kansas State Historical Society* 15 (1919–1922).

Hafen, LeRoy, and Ann W. Hafen, eds. *Relations with the Indians of the*

Plains, 1857–1861: A Documentary Account. In LeRoy R. Hafen, *The Far West and Rockies Series*, vol. 9. Glendale, CA: Arthur H. Clark Company, 1959.

Hafen, LeRoy, W. Eugene Hollon, and Carl Coke Rister. *Western America.* Englewood Cliffs, NJ: Prentice-Hall, Inc., 3rd ed., 1970.

Haines, Francis. *The Buffalo.* New York: Thomas Y. Crowell Company, 1970.

Halaas, David Fridjof and Andrew E. Masich. *Halfbreed: The Remarkable True Story of George Bent—Caught Between Worlds of the Indian and the White Man.* Cambridge, MA: De Capo Press, 2005.

Haley, J. Evatts. "The Comanchero Trade." *Southwestern Historical Quarterly* 38, no. 3 (January 1935).

Hämäläinen, Pekka. *The Comanche Empire.* New Haven: Yale University Press, 2008.

———. "The Western Comanche Trade Center: Rethinking the Plains Indian Trade System." *Western Hisorical Quarterly* 29, no. 4 (Winter 1998).

Hammond, George P. *The Adventures of Alexander Barclay, Mountain Man.* Denver: Old West Publishing Company, 1976.

Hill, Eward E. *The Office of Indian Affairs, 1824–1880.* New York: Clearwater Publishing Company, 1974.

Hobbs, James. *Wild Life in the Far West: Personal Adventures of a Border Man.* Facsimile reprint of the 1872 edition. Alexandra, VA: Time-Life Books, 1980.

Hyde, George E. *Life of George Bent Written from his Letters.* Ed. Savoie Lottinville. Norman: University of Oklahoma press, 1968.

Hyslop, Stephen G. *Bound for Santa Fe: The Road to New Mexico and the American Conquest, 1806–1848.* Norman: University of Oklahoma Press, 2002.

Inman, Colonel Henry. *The Old Santa Fe Trail: The Story of a Great Highway.* Topeka: Crane and Company, 1899.

Isenberg, Andrew C. *The Destruction of the Bison: An Environmental History, 1750–1920.* New York: Cambridge University Press, 2000.

———. "The Market Revolution in the Borderlands: George C. Sibley in Missouri and New Mexico, 1808–1826." *Journal of the Early Republic* 21, no. 3 (Autumn 2001).

Isern, Thomas D., ed. "Exploration and Diplomacy: Geoge Champlin Sibley's Report to William Clark." *Missouri Historical Review* 73, no. 1 (October 1978).

Jackson, Donald. "Journey to the Mandans, 1809: The Lost Narrative of Dr. Thomas." Missouri Historical Society *Bulletin* 10, no. 3 (April 1964).

Jablow, Joseph. *The Cheyennes in Plains Indian Trade Relations, 1795–1840*. New York: J. J. Augustin, 1951.

Karnes, Thomas L. "Gilpin's Volunteers on the Santa Fe Trail." *Kansas Historical Quarterly* 30, no. 3 (September 1962).

Kavanagh, Thomas W. *The Comanches: A History, 1707–1875*. Lincoln: University of Nebraska Press, 1996.

Klunder, Willard Carl. *Lewis Cass and the Politics of Moderation*. Kent, OH: Kent State University Press, 1996.

Lecompte, Janet. "Gantt's Fort and Bent's Picket Post." *Colorado Magazine* 41, no. 2, (Spring 1964).

———. *Pueblo, Hardscrabble, Greenhorn: The Upper Arkansas, 1832–1856*. Norman: University of Oklahoma Press, 1978.

Manning, William R. "Diplomacy Concerning the Santa Fe Road." *Mississippi Valley Historical Review* 1 (March 1915).

Meline, James F. *Two Thousand Miles on Horseback, Santa Fe and Back: A Summer Tour through Kansas, Nebraska, Colorado, and New Mexico, in the Year 1866*. New York: Hurd and Houghton, 1867.

Miner, H. Craig and William E. Unrau. *The End of Indian Kansas: A History of Cultural Revolution, 1854–1871*. Lawrence: Regents Press of Kansas, 1978.

———. *The St. Louis-San Franciso Transcontinental Railroad: The Thirty-Fifth Parallel Project, 1853–1890*. Lawrence: University Press of Kansas, 1972.

Morse, Rev. Jedidiah. *Report to the Secretary of War of the United States on Indian Affairs, Comprising a Narrative of Tour Performed in the Summer of 1820*. New Haven: S. Converse, 1822.

Nichols, Roger L. *General Henry Atkinson: A Western Military Career*. Norman: University of Oklahoma Press, 1965.

Perrine, Fred S., ed. "Hugh Evans' Journal of Colonel Henry Dodge's Expedition to the Rocky Mountains in 1835." *Mississippi Valley Historical Review* 14, no. 2 (September 1927).

Oglesby, Richard Edward. *Manuel Lisa and the Opening of the Missouri Fur Trade*. Norman: University of Oklahoma Press, 1963.

Oliva, Leo E. "Fort Atkinson on the Santa Fe Trail, 1850–1854." *Kansas Historical Quarterly* 40, no. 2 (Summer 1974).

———. *Soldiers on the Santa Fe Trail*. Norman: University of Oklahoma Press, 1967.

Oswald, Delmont R. (introduction and notes). *The Life and Adventures of James P. Beckworth as Told to Thomas D. Bonner*. Lincoln: University of Nebraska Press, 1972.

Phillips, Paul Chrisler. *The Fur Trade*. 2 vols. Norman: University of Oklahoma Press, 1961.

Powell, Peter J. *Sweet Medicine: The Continuing Role of the Sacred Arrows, the Sun Dance, and the Sacred Buffalo Hat in Northern Cheyenne History*. 2 vols. Norman: University of Oklahoma Press, 1969.

Prucha, Francis Paul. *American Indian Treaties: The History of a Political Anomaly*. Berkeley: University of California Press, 1994.

———. *American Indian Policy in the Formative Years: The Indian Trade and Intercourse Acts, 1790–1834*. Cambridge: Harvard University Press, 1962.

Reséndez, Andrés. "Getting Cured and Getting Drunk: State vs. Market in Texas and New Mexico, 1800–1850." *Journal of the Early Republic* 22, no. 1 (Spring 2002).

Richmond, Robert W. *Kansas: A Land of Contrasts*. Arlington Heights, IL: Forum Press, 3rd ed., 1989.

Rorabaugh, W. J. *The Alcoholic Republic*. New York: Oxford University Press, 1979.

Ruxton, Geo. F. *Adventures in New Mexico and the Rocky Mountains*. London: John Murray, 1849.

Sabin, Edward Lagrand. *Kit Carson Days (1809-1868)*. Chicago: A. C. McClurg and Co., 1914.

Sage, Rufus B. *Rocky Mountain Life; or Startling and Perilous Adventures in the Far West*. Dayton, OH: Edward Canby, 1846.

Sandoz, Mari. *The Buffalo Men: the Story of the Hide Men*. New York: Hastings House, 1954.

Sayles, Stephen. "Thomas Hart Benton and the Santa Fe Trail." *Missouri Historical Review* 69, no. 1 (October 1974).

Sherow, James E. "Workings of the Geodialectic: High Plains Indians and their Horses in the Region of the Arkansas River Vallley, 1800–1870." *Environmental History Review* 16, no. 2 (Summer 1992).

Simmons, Marc. *On the Santa Fe Trail*. Lawrence: University Press of Kansas, 1986.

———. *The Old Santa Fe Trail: Collected Essays*. Albuquerque: University of New Mexico Press, 1996.

Smith, Elbert B. *Magnificent Missourian: Thomas Hart Benton*. Philadelphia: Lippencott, 1957.

Smith, Henry Nash. *Virgin Land: The American West as Myth and Symbol*. Cambridge: Harvard University Press, 1978.

Socolofsky, Homer E., and Huber Self. *Historical Atlas of Kansas*. Norman: University of Oklahoma Press, 1972.

Stanley, Henry M. *My Early Travels in America and Asia*. London: Gerald Duckworth and Co., 2001.

Steckmesser, Kent Ladd. *The Westward Movement: A Short History*. New York: McGraw-Hill, Inc., 1969.

Steffen, Jerome O. *William Clark: Jeffersonian Man on the Frontier*. Norman: University of Oklahoma Press, 1977.

Steiger, John W. "Benjamin O'Fallon." In LeRoy R. Hafen (ed.), *The Mountain Men and the Fur Trade of the Far West*, vol. 5. Glendale, CA: Arthur H. Clark Company, 1968.

Stein, Gary C. "A Fearful Drunkenness: The Liquor Trade to the Western Indians as Seen by European Travellers in America, 1800–1860." *Red River Valley Historical Review, 1800–1869* 1 (Summer 1974).

Stoddard, Amos. *Sketches, Historical, and Descriptive of Louisiana*. Philadelphia: Matthew Carey, 1812.

Taylor, Morris F. *First Mail West: Stagecoach Lines on the Santa Fe Trail*. Albuquerque: University of New Mexico Press, 1971.

Trennert, Robert A. Jr. *Alternative to Extinction: Federal Indian Policy and the Beginning of the Reservation System*. Philadelphia: Temple University Press, 1976.

———. "Indian Policy on the Santa Fe Road: The Fitzpatrick Controversy." *Kansas History* 1, no. 4 (Winter 1978).

Unrau, William E. "George C. Sibley's Plea for the 'Garden of Missouri' in 1824." Missouri Historical Society *Bulletin* 8, no. 1 (October 1970).

———. "Indian Agent v. the Army: Some Background Notes of the Kiowa-Comanche Treaty of 1865." *Kansas Historical Quarterly* 30, no. 2 (Summer 1962).

———. *Indians of Kansas: The Euro-American Conquest of Indian Kansas*. Topeka: Kansas State Historical Society, 1991.

———. "The Depopulation of the Dheghia-Siouan Kansas Prior to Removal." *New Mexico Historical Review* 48, no. 4 (October 1973).

———. *The Kansa Indians: A History of the Wind People, 1673–1873*. Norman: University of Oklahoma Press, 1971.

———. *The Rise and Fall of Indian Country, 1825–1855*. Lawrence: University Press of Kansas, 2007.

———. *White Man's Wicked Water: The Alcohol Trade and Prohibition in Indian Country, 1802–1892*. Lawrence: University Press of Kansas, 1996.

Unruh, John D. Jr. *The Plains Across: The Overland Emigrants and the Trans-Mississippi West*. Urbana: University of Illinois Press, 1979.

Van Meter, Sondra. *Marion County Kansas: Past and Present*. Marion, KS: Marion County Historical Society, 1972.

Viola, Herman J. *Thomas L. McKenney: Architect of America's Early Indian Policy, 1816–1830*. Chicago: Swallow Press, 1974.

Voelker, Frederic F. "Ezekiel Williams of Boon's Lick." Missouri Historical Society *Bulletin* 8, no. 1 (October 1951).

Walker, Henry P. *The Wagonmasters: High Plains Freighting from Earliest Days of the Santa Fe Trail to 1880*. Norman: University of Oklahoma Press, 1966.

Way, Peter. "Evil Humors and Ardent Spirits: The Rough Culture of Canal Construction Workers." *Journal of American History* 79, no. 2 (March 1993).

Weber, David J. *The Taos Trappers: The Fur Trade of the Far Southwest, 1540–1846*. Norman: University of Oklahoma Press, 1971.

———. "American Westward Expansion and the Breakdown of Relations Between Pobladores and 'Indio Barbaros' on Mexico's Far NorthernJ Frontier, 1821–1846." *New Mexico Historical Review* 56, no. 3 (1981).

West, Elliott. *The Contested Plains: Indians, Goldseekers, and the Rush to Colorado*. Lawrence: University Press of Kansas, 1998.

Wishart, David J. *The Fur Trade of the Amerian West, 1807–1840: A Geographical Synthesis*. Lincoln: University of Nebraska Press, 1979.

Wilson, Elinor. *Jim Beckworth: Black Mountain Man and War Chief of the Crows*. Norman: University of Oklahoma Press, 1955.

White, Richard. *"It's your Misfortune and None of My Own": A History of the American West*. Norman: University of Oklahoma Press, 1991.

Williams, Ezekiel (letter). "Ezekiel Williams' Adventures in Colorado." Missouri Historical Society *Collections* 4, no. 2 (1913).

Wohl, R. Richard. "Three Generations of Business Enterprise in a Midwestern City: The McGees of a Kansas City." *Journal of Economic History* 16 (1956).

Wyman, Walker D. "Freighting: A Big Business on the Santa Fe Trail." *Kansas Historical Quarterly* 1 (November 1931).

Index